this book is for the children

Arin, Brooks and Peter

Word Wheel Books   Menlo Park California

EGGS & PEANUT BUTTER

a teacher's scrapbook

written by David Weitzman
and designed by
James Robertson

Copyright © 1974 by David Weitzman
All rights reserved
Library of Congress Catalog Card Number: 74—83651
ISBN: 0—913700—02—9

First printing: November 1974
Printed in the United States of America

This book was designed and prepared for publication
at The Yolla Bolly Press in Covelo California
during September and October 1974.

Word Wheel Books, Inc.
Post Office Box 441
Menlo Park, California 94025

"Who am I?," pp.31-33, from *More Comics for Teachers (and kids)*. Copyright © 1974 by Marilyn Burns and James Robertson. Reprinted by permission of the Amazing Life Games Company.

"A Worker Reads History," p.34, from *Selected Poems of Bertolt Brecht*, translated by H. R. Hays, copyright © 1947 by Bertolt Brecht and H. R. Hays. Reprinted by permission of Harcourt Brace Jovanovich, Inc.

"The Playful Mood," p.37, from *The Ordeal of Change* (1963) by Eric Hoffer. Copyright © by Eric Hoffer. By permission of Harper & Row, Publishers, Inc.

Excerpt, p.40, abridged by permission of William Morrow & Co., Inc. from *Blackberry Winter* by Margaret Mead. Copyright © 1972 by Margaret Mead.

"Getting it All Together," p.61, from *Asian Thought* Teacher's Manual by John U. Michaelis and Robin J. McKeown, pp.10, 11, 12, 13, 14. From the *Asian Studies Inquiry Program*. Copyright © 1969 by Field Educational Publications, Inc. Reprinted by permission of Addison-Wesley Publishing Company, Inc.

"Are You All Right?," p.38, and "Fire the Cannon," p.69, from *Hear the Sound of My Feet Walking* by Dan O'Neill. By permission of Glide Publications. Copyright © 1969 by Chronicle Publishing Company

Excerpt, p.81, from *Technology and Change* by Donald A. Schon. Copyright © 1967 by Donald A. Schon. Used with permission of Delacorte Press/ Seymour Lawrence.

"Weitzman's Funky Fossils," p.101, excerpt from *The Human Experience* by David Weitzman and Richard E. Gross. Copyright © 1974 by Houghton Mifflin Company. Used by permission of Houghton Mifflin Company.

"Art in a Cultural Context," p.115, adapted with permission of Macmillan Publishing Co. Inc. from *Cultural and Social Anthropology* by Peter B. Hammond. Copyright © 1971 by Peter B. Hammond.

"Playboy Interview with Marshall McLuhan," p.124. Originally appeared in Playboy magazine; copyright © 1969 by Playboy.

"Uses of the Past: A Framework for Speculation," p.136, reprinted with permission of Macmillan Publishing Co., from *The Year 2000* by Herman Kahn and Anthony J. Wiener. Copyright © 1967 by The Hudson Institute, Inc.

Contents

HE WHO BINDS TO HIMSELF A JOY DOES THE WINGED LIFE DESTROY

This is about the winged lives of teachers, and kids, and schools, changing, fluttering in and out of each other's consciousness, and crashing from the now into the future. But, then, it's easy to say what a book's all about; what is infinitely more difficult is to make it really about that.

What this book is really about is my own struggle with change. I began with confidence. After all, I've been teaching for ten years now, watching myself and others going through all sorts of changes. I've watched teachers changing into different kinds of teachers and teachers not changing into different kinds of teachers, university students changing into teachers, my own children changing into students and me desperately trying to change them back into children once again, schools changing, parents changing, and even—though this requires patience and time-lapse perceptions—principals and superintendents changing. I've been there and I understand; or so I thought. Because when I set about really doing it, I found out just how elusive the mechanisms and motivations for change really are.

BUT HE WHO KISSES THE JOY AS IT FLIES LIVES IN ETERNITY'S SUN RISE.

There are in books about change inherent contradictions, like trying to express the process in words, particularly the printed word. Change will just not stand still to be grasped and be described, and certainly will not be stilled long enough to be frozen into type and contained by covers. Words like CHANGE printed on a page become static images which bear no resemblance to the dynamic processes they are meant to describe. So it became clear that there were going to be some real problems writing a book, or whatever, on change. Any device that might be used to express and to define the movement from now to tomorrow would at the same time be shaped by the very process it

7

seeks to capture, in the same way that the space around an object also describes its shape and is, in turn, re-shaped by movement and changes in the object. The medium of expression I chose, then, would not only have to be adapted, formed around the peculiar nature of the subject—change—but would have to be supple enough to move with and define as clearly as possible the subtle, all but invisible movements and changes going on underneath. I suppose my discovery must be like those earliest attempts to learn about air. At first, no one even thought to ask about air because it doesn't seem to exist; we are totally unaware of it. Unaware until we try to contain it in some way, to give it boundaries, like a bag, for example. The bag makes us suddenly aware of air as a substance, filling the bag and giving it shape. If we close off the bag, isolate the air inside, we realize that not only doesn't the bag collapse, there is actually something inside. If we heat the air it expands and draws the surface of the bag taut; cooling the bag makes the air contract and the surface of the bag becomes looser. We still have not seen the substance we've captured; but we know it's there because it shapes its container, and by observing we've learned something of its properties. Change is like that.

All of which suggests to me some ways of looking at students and teachers changing, and something of the shape of this book. The fragile, vaporous nature of the subject means that it's not to be studied, mulled over, done to death; a book about change should be spontaneous, and because a book is never more than a moment in the time of the author's life it should not take much longer than that to do. Its sections, rather than chapters, will be experiences and moments in time, and were I able to do so in a way we could all understand I'd have no divisions or headings at all! The images, because they are fleeting, will only be sketched in, capturing some thought or action in a few strokes, just enough to convey the movement and feeling, in much the same way that a photographer lets the moving image blur to show its motion. It is a pointillist technique, revealing moments of light and color upon close inspection, blending into an overall image of change when viewed from farther away, with perspective rather than analysis, with reverie instead of intense thought. Space is not time in this book as it is in most; it is simply different places and spaces without any linearity.

Anyway, this is a book about change, not change *away from* the public school as in private alterna-

tive schools, but change toward new kinds of teaching in public schools. I grew up in a city, attended city schools, and have always taught in city schools; I think they are the most exciting places to learn and in which to teach, and they offer opportunities for personal discovery and interpersonal relationships that we haven't begun to consider. I want them to survive and grow. But not at any cost. Every other aspect of American life is undergoing an incredible metamorphosis, and there is something strangely out of step about a school or faculty that refuses to accept this fact. If, like other useless, unadaptive organisms in the universe, schools cannot accommodate the needs of children in a world in which change is and will continue to be the only constant, then the schools must die. If they do we must accept those consequences and assume the responsibility for that event. Despite the constant reference to "them," the specters who conspire against everything we do, both what ails public schools and all that is needed to heal them and make them grow is *within* us. There are only three things that could destroy public schools and public education: failure to keep up with the rapid changes of the technological world; failure to recognize and adopt new techniques and materials and draw from any new area of knowledge which has something to offer; and failure of teachers to free themselves from the constraints of their preconceptions about schools and kids.

You may be puzzled by some of the things in this book and wonder, for example, why a book about teaching should include games, or readings on media, or kite-flying contests, or primitive art, or predictions for the future, or mingle social studies, mathematics, science, and language skills in the same context. Well, change cannot take place as long as teachers continue to be prisoners of their own preconceptions of what schools are, what the role of the teacher is, what kinds of things should go on in a classroom or a school, how schools fit into life, who young people are, how they feel about themselves and others around them, and what they want from school—and even preconceptions about their own potential for growth and change and adaptability. It's not that teachers are *unable* to change; teachers don't change because they don't *believe* they can and they're afraid of what they'll discover about themselves and others if they do change. And this is the most constricting of all—the inability of teachers to see themselves doing new things under new cir-

8

cumstances, being something different from what they imagine themselves to be when something different is needed.

Change exists nowhere but in ourselves. The struggle with change is a very personal struggle, and while we may talk of "institutions changing" what we are really talking about is people changing and causing institutions to change.

We've gone to great lengths to avoid facing that fact and all its implications. We blame our failings on a lack of money; but what would we do with it if we had it? It is interesting that not one book I've found on the dynamics of change says anything about spending more money; the emphasis is always on the human beings in the system, particularly those closest to the process to be changed. Teachers' organizations continue to expend great energies pounding away at state legislatures, politicians, school boards, superintendents, and administrators, having failed to learn after all this time one discomforting but very real fact: the farther you are from the classroom the less influence you have on change in the classroom. Change will occur when *teachers* want change and make it happen, and not until then. Change cannot be legislated, mandated, or promoted with posters and superintendent's bulletins. Nor will it come with a "new" principal or superintendent. How many times have you waited anxiously for your new principal to make change happen in the school, or watched hopefully the election or appointment of a new superintendent who seems to know all the right words, only to find that he's powerless to make any changes? Each moves on his way, leaving little imprint, if any, on their giant bureaucracies, systems which, far from encouraging change, are actually designed to stifle it. We've rooted out virtually every bogeyman, pointed the finger at all the scapegoats, identified all the external influences on schools that we say prevent change or hurt schools, doing everything we can to avoid thinking about what we should be thinking about and coming back to the most uncomfortable (and, therefore, the closest to home) thought of all—*change* happens in the classroom, and it is the teacher who makes it happen.

Change resides within us. So when I began to look for some of the mechanisms of change I didn't look at organization charts or the "institution" in its most political and abstract sense; I looked at change in the only place I have learned that it can be found, with the individual teacher who has devel-

oped a personal strategy for change. I simply turned to four other teachers in my school and watched how they have made their classrooms a change space. One is a woman, three are men. Faye Das, Ron Valentine, and I have been teaching about ten years; Bob Falk for about four, and Bill Ames for less than a year. For all of us, virtually our total teaching experience has been in large urban schools. None of us is a magician or possesses any superhuman powers. While my selection is certainly not random, I have no reason to believe that the five of us happening at one school wasn't random (we're probably the most random five people you'll ever meet). Certainly our methods are very different.

Change does not mean that we always have to be moving toward something "new." Change can mean very simply an interesting twist to an old idea. In fact, none of the ideas in this book is in the least revolutionary. If we acknowledge that Bill borrowed his videotape hardware (thank you Harry Stehr and Don Hatfield) and that many districts have similar equipment tucked away somewhere, then I can point out that none of the models described in this book costs more than some cardboard, paint, paper plates, several boxes of toothpicks, a few feet of scrap wood, an occasional bus trip, and very little time (Ron comes up with incredible ideas on the spot on Monday mornings). Five Squares was borrowed from some anonymous analyst somewhere; it's probably as old as the study of psychology. Bob's blocks came from some wood pile, and the idea is as old as folding dollar bills to support glasses of water. Faye's masks go back at least 50,000 years, and Ron's projects, though they look like something from the Armory Show, actually go back to the Bauhaus tradition of problem solving with natural materials. Only Bill's medium seems very new, but not when you consider that many schools have been using 8 mm stuff for years. And, of course, assembling fossils has been done before; my way is just a little less messy.

Finally, it needs to be said that our book is nowhere near complete, nor could it ever be. Our intention is not to instruct but to reach out, to touch ideas, to be part of and contribute to a growing consciousness among kids and teachers, to share. Somewhere among these pages are chapters yet to be written describing more of that consciousness, ultimately the most valid chapters of all—your own.

Your Education

There is a world of difference between the modern home environment of integrated electric information and the classroom. Today's television child is attuned to up-to-the-minute "adult" news—inflation, rioting, war, taxes, crime, bathing beauties—and is bewildered when he enters the nineteenth-century environment that still characterizes the educational establishment where information is scarce but ordered and structured by fragmented, classified patterns, subjects, and schedules. It is naturally an environment much like any factory set-up with its inventories and assembly lines.

The "child" was an invention of the seventeenth century; he did not exist in, say, Shakespeare's day. He had, up until that time, been merged in the adult world and there was nothing that could be called childhood in our sense.

Today's child is growing up absurd, because he lives in two worlds, and neither of them inclines him to grow up. Growing up—that is our new work, and it is *total*. Mere instruction will not suffice.

Marshall McLuhan

IT WAS

ALL HAPPEN ING AT ONCE!

And it wouldn't stop. The two announcements could hardly have been less dramatic, coming as they did during a week when most Americans watched with an acute sense of deja vu—if they watched at all—the final Apollo flight and moon-landing. Against the staged surrealism of the launch preparations and the labored, self-conscious "excitement" of TV anchormen and retired astronauts who had almost begun pleading with us to delight in an event which no longer interested us, the *San Francisco Chronicle* proclaimed "The Oldest Man Unearthed" and a few pages back "A New Life for Creation." The first story announced Richard Leakey's discovery of a skull belonging to a man of the genus Homo who lived over 2.5 million years ago, half a million years older than the skull of Homo habilis discovered by his father. The second story, under the heading "education," described attempts by the Creation Science Research Center to influence members of the California State Curriculum Commission to mandate the teaching of biblical creation in grades 1 through 8, requiring that publishers include the story of Genesis in science texts submitted for adoption in the state. In an issue covered with an insipid ski-bunny and the banner HOLIDAY ON SKIS/ THE HOTTEST SPORT, THE COOLEST SLOPES, *Time* editors buried the article "Apollo 17: A Grand Finale" on page 30. On the next page appeared an article evoking the 1925 Scopes "monkey trial," asking in its title "Darwin Who?". And there was the austere visage of the evolutionist himself, his head turned away in affront, ignoring that impertinent, rhetorical question behind him, seemingly engrossed in another, boldfaced heading directly in line of his sight—DRAMA OF SOULS.

WHILE STROLLING ON THE MOON ONE DAY

(scenario for a happening in four simultaneous scenes)

an earth/space/fantasy/reality based on actual events and direct quotations reported in the *San Francisco Chronicle* and *Time* (December, 1972)

cast of characters

(in order of reincarnation and appearance)

Charles Darwin	naturalist, eminent Victorian, and author of *On the Origin of Species*
Nell Seagraves	founder and spokeswoman of Creation Science Research Center
Jack Schmitt	astronaut, Harvard-trained geologist
Gene Cernan	astronaut
Richard Leakey	anthropologist
Dr. John Ford	physician, member California State Board of Education
Dr. Thomas H. Jukes	biochemist, UC Berkeley
chorus	Glenn T. Seaborg, Harold C. Urey, Linus Pauling, Willard F. Libby, and several other Nobel prizewinners.

[revolving stage, divided into four sets described below, is dark and revolves to present each scene as a speaker is cued. A spot lights scene for duration of lines. It is sometime during the month of December, 1972]

1

[scene 1: Taurus-Littrow valley of the Moon. Above the jagged peaks of moon mountains the planet earth can be seen in the background]

2

[scene 2: somewhere on an east African savanna; scrub brush dots endless open spaces receding into the background, empty but for a Land Rover to the side]

With a Land-Rover, you can rub elbows with the natives of New England. Or New Guinea.

Schmitt: [excited] A geologist's paradise if I've ever seen one!

Cernan: [lunges at a moon rock with his geologist's hammer and accidentally smashes fender off of moon vehicle] Dadgummit!

3

[scene 3: a meeting room of the California State Curriculum Commission in the state capital, Sacramento]

4

[scene 4: Charles Darwin's study and laboratory cluttered with specimens of birds and scientific apparatus]

Darwin: [seated amidst a clutter of fossils, stuffed birds, and scribbled notes] In the beginning God created heaven and earth . . .

Seagraves: At present the evolutionists own the system and they're crying because they have to give it up . . .

Darwin: And the earth was without form and darkness was upon the face of the deep; and the spirit of God moved upon the waters . . .

Darwin: And God said: Let there be light and there was light . . . .

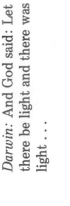

Teacher: [reading from school textbook] "It is known that life began in the seas . . . .

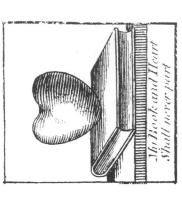

My Book and Heart
Shall never part

Leakey: [speaking from his Land Rover] . . . clear evidence that in eastern Africa a large-brained, truly upright and bipedal form of genus Homo existed . . . more than 2.5 million years ago . . . It is almost certainly the oldest complete skull of early man . . .

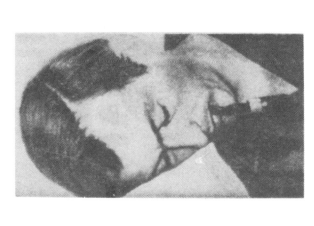

Leakey: [holding fossil skull] The whole shape of the brain case is remarkably reminiscent of modern man . . . .

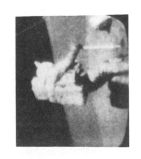

Schmitt: [kicking around in the moon dust] Hey, there is orange soil. It's all over . . .

Cernan: [chugging over toward Schmitt] Well, don't move until I see it.

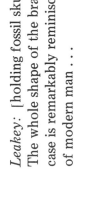

Schmitt: I still haven't learned how to pick up rocks . . . a very embarrassing thing for a geologist to admit.

Darwin: And God said, Let the waters bring forth abundantly the moving creature that hath life and fowl that may fly above the earth . . .

Teacher: [working up a draft on scratch paper] How about "*Scientists believe* that life began in the seas?"

Leakey: [holding the giant leg-bone of a woolly mammoth] The leg bones have astounded anatomists and other scientists because they are practically indistinguishable from the same bones of modern man . . .

Cernan: [has just fallen over and is struggling to get up] Dadgummit!

Seagraves: As I often kiddingly state, we're asking for 50 per cent of the education system back. At one time we owned it all!

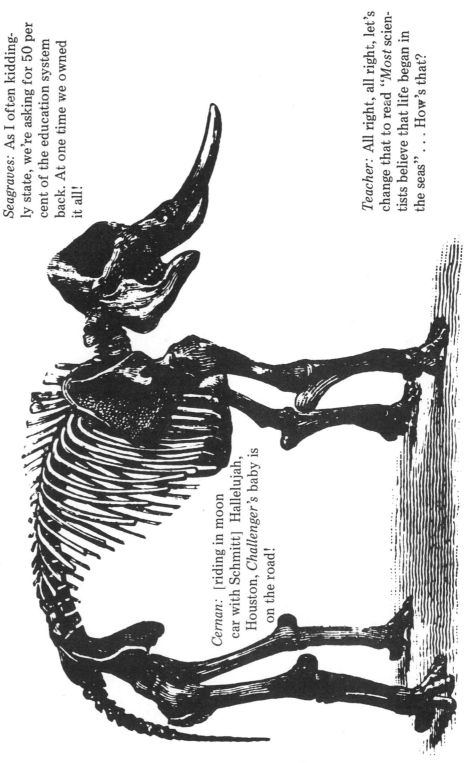

Cernan: [riding in moon car with Schmitt] Hallelujah, Houston, *Challenger's* baby is on the road!

Teacher: All right, all right, let's change that to read "*Most* scientists believe that life began in the seas" . . How's that?

Darwin: And God created whales and every living creature that moveth....

Jukes: Transitional forms are not absent. We can detect them by using new procedures of molecular evolution, discovered within the past few years....

Teacher: [exasperated but determined] "*Most scientists believe that life may have begun in the seas.*"

Chorus: [chanting in a Gregorian mode] Conditional statements are appropriate when multiple theories have been proposed and none of these can be eliminated by existing scientific evidence....

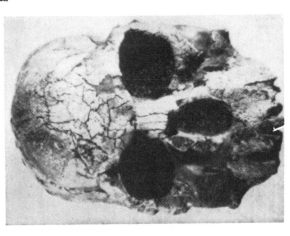

THE SKULL (PATCHED UP) FROM EAST AFRICA
It was very similar to modern man's

Schmitt: [pretending that he is skiing] Whoosh! Whoosh! Wheeee! Little hard to get good hip rotation....

Schmitt: [picking up moon rocks and putting them in plastic bags] I feel like a kid playing in a sandbox.

A Man of the Herds

Cernan and Schmitt: [dancing clumsily, constricted by their EVA suits] . . . While strolling on the moon one day . . . in the merry month of December

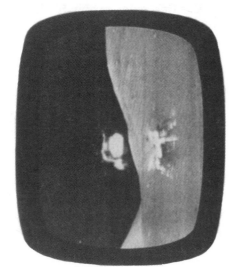

Jukes: A single drop of blood contains chemical information telling us that we are closely related to the chimpanzee and gorilla, not so closely to horses and cattle, and more distantly, step by step, to kangaroos, chickens, frogs, and bony fishes . . .

Darwin: So God created man in His own image . . . .

Leakey: While the skull is different from our own species, Homo sapiens, it is also different from all other known forms of early man . . . .

Chorus: No alternative to the evolutionary theory gives an equally satisfactory explanation of the biological facts.

. . . and thus does not fit into any of the presently held theories of human evolution.

Darwin: Dadgummit!

[As Darwin buries his head in the clutter of his desk, multi-colored strobe lights flash and the stage begins to revolve faster, becoming a December evolution biblical kaleidoscope]

Structure Is Freedom

You should know at the outset that I like structure. I like structure because it makes possible knowing and understanding, adapting, dealing with challenging or threatening things, becoming accustomed to, even comfortable with, the new, the unexperienced, the unexpected, the uncertain. But when I use the word I mean it in a sense different from the way it is usually used. I mean it in the sense of the way people put things together in their heads, think, decide, speculate, guess, and make assumptions that allow them to go on to the next step. Structure in a class, or anywhere, is a fragile, intuitive, natural quality that disappears when we become too aware and too self-conscious, when we try to analyze and define it. It becomes awkward when we think too much about it, when we try to expose it each step along the way, when we try to make a thing of it. It's not something to be slavishly sought after or worshiped. It is not a trick or an intellectual gadget. But it *is* an inherent part of everything we do, every conscious process

like learning, or exploring, or problem-solving, just thinking, or even creating. Biographies of artists, composers, writers, thinkers, all kinds of creative people, reveal very different and very personal schemes or strategies, or structures, or whatever you want to call it, for doing the things they want to do.

And this is one of the dilemmas of trying to talk about something like structure; although it's so elemental and so natural, it doesn't seem to be innate but needs to be acquired or learned in some way. For the longest time I just didn't know what to do about this. I knew from experience that structure could not be "taught," certainly not in the usual sense of that word, anyway—and yet nothing really happens if you leave it all to chance. But the acquiring of a structure for thinking can happen; I've seen it happen on lots of occasions with all kinds of kids, and it happens not fortuitously, but intuitively. It doesn't happen when teachers lack structure themselves. It cannot be imparted

18

in a didactic way. No amount of talking about structure, analyzing, outlining it in five or twelve or twenty easy foolproof steps, is going to do it. Structure is something sensed, felt, detected in others.

I think that if a child lacks structure in dealing with problems, say, or in approaching some task, or just in the way he does all kinds of things, he can be helped to develop thinking structure of his own. I've noticed that students who are unable to think in an orderly way are acutely aware—painfully aware—of others who can. This awareness is the first step—creating a kind of anxiety or motivation for getting it together like the others. This is, in fact, what many of us mean when we say that we have sensed in our children a desire for order, for some kind of structure, or more than that, a quest, a longing for an orderly way to look at the world.

Structure is a state of mind. Structure is a comfortable way of doing things. There are many kinds of structure that vary because people are different, many ways of doing things that each of us must learn for ourselves because, despite that initial conscious effort that seems so unnatural, they will eventually provide us with a system of solving problems, finding information, organizing and ordering things, of doing something useful, creative, or helpful to others, or merely a way to be happier. The reward for structure is freedom, and while you may not be able to accept this fact where you are now, there can be no freedom, no creative thought, without structure—not artificial, impersonal, imposed structure from without, but an inherent, internalized, personal structure emerging from within. Once I realized this, the next step, the much more difficult step, was finding a way to do something about it.

First of all, even in large, diverse faculties like the one of which I am a part there is an almost universal recognition of the need for structure. It is, in fact, one of the few things that faculties seem to be able to agree upon. But here the harmony stops, because the next question—what the hell you do about it—is the killer, the sure way to break up any orderly teacher's meeting into screaming, brawling chaos. After ten years of such meetings I think I've learned something: the words "structure" and "order" not only have two larger meanings for people but the meanings also happen to be absolutely irreconcilable, almost unbridgeable antitheses. At this point we could get into sticky discussions involving classification of these views into dichotomies like existentialism versus benevolent paternalism, or the free versus the ordered society.

But I think there's a simpler way to approach structure which, if not accurate, is at least useful. The problem arises from the inability to discriminate between what at first seems to be a very subtle distinction, between what I will call *structure as environment* and *structure as state of mind*. It comes down to this: is structure an environment, a climate that compels people to act in orderly, structured ways, or is it an internal thing, a state of mind which radiates outward to create a sense of structure and orderly behavior?

Structure as environment is, I believe, what most teachers and parents refer to when they attempt to describe the orderly learning process they seek. Structure as environment is usually expressed in some variant of the idea that "things must be structured" for the child, things are to be arranged, planned, set up, coordinated, worked out, directed, channeled, pre-conceived as to form, process, and direction. The syntax of this thought is significant, because it makes clear that structure is something external to the child—events and circumstances created by adults, teachers in this context, who presumably have a notion of structure and set about making it happen. In this scheme of structure there is someone in control, manipulating the context, behavior, and environment of someone else. Without getting heavy, I think it likely that this "external" concept of structure comes from our failure or inability to detect structure within ourselves. In

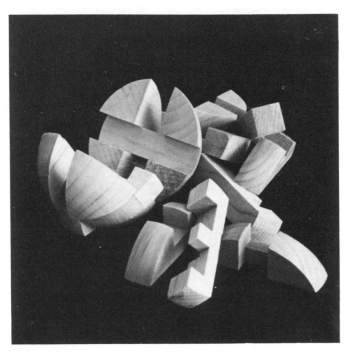

other words, it is the illusive, subconscious, quality of structure within ourselves that leads us to conclude that it must be the product of some external thing existing somewhere outside of us. We seem to project our own sense of internal order out to where we think we can deal with it. Or we may refuse to accept the fact that it is indeed something we have acquired and internalized. But in either case the effect is to attribute it to external events and other people. But it needn't be so abstract. I can give an actual example from my own experiences at school.

Occasionally—though not nearly often enough—the state of mind of our students becomes the subject of a faculty meeting. I hear teachers saying that our students need a structure, a sense of direction, an orderly learning environment, a less variable environment that lets students feel more comfortable and secure. I agree with this. They go on to say, then, that students need this order and structure because so much of their lives is disordered, a disorder not to be confused with freedom but a kind of disorder which is everything but freedom, uncomfortable, confusing, enervating, and eventually fatal to any real sense of direction. I agree with this also. But then someone says that *we* are the responsible adults in this school—responsible in ways of maturity, experience, and foresight—which gives us the right to determine (to structure) the direction, objectives, and goals of each child. Here the logic begins to unravel. And now is when structure as environment gets defined, in the recommen-

dations offered to meet these needs: strict tardy rules (and punishment for teachers and students who fail to comply), better procedures for reporting offenders, stricter attendance rules, more suspensions, more blue-slips, pink-slips, golden-rod slips, notes from home, clamping down, tightening up, no more "permissiveness," let 'em know who's

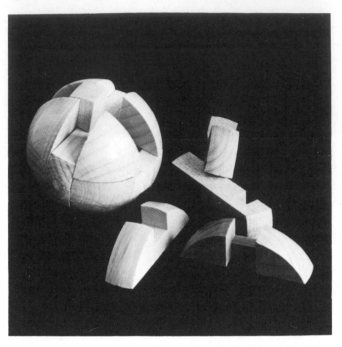

boss, get tough, no shades and no hats, more locker inspections, lock up the doors, hire more hall-ranging gestapo, send more kids to the vice principals, gangbusters, call the cops, lock the johns, keep them in line! Of course, as you've noticed, we've ceased long ago talking about "structure." Nothing in any of this fulfills or even begins to meet the needs of students, the need for *internal* structure and security, an orderliness inside the mind, inside the soul, or wherever comfort and self-confidence reside in us. None of this creates an environment where children can experience the *feeling* of security, where real structure can even begin to happen. Not only is this kind of thing counterproductive to the development of any real structure in learning, it is in itself, sadly, an example of unstructured, irrational, and unworkable behavior on the part of supposedly "responsible" adults.

"Structure" is something we can share but cannot impose. Structure is something that can be experienced by any child but not planned for him, and certainly not crammed down his throat. It is not external to the student. My structure is not your structure. Structure is not adherence or conformity. One does not create a structured, free

mind through strictness, arbitrary rules, demands and rewards. The teacher who methodically plans out each moment of the lesson or makes sure everybody is busy every moment of the class period, who spends more time on tardy and absence slips than talking to kids, who insensitively passes over real problems in little lives, who ignores relevant and interesting diversions, or who charges ahead, blind to subtle and frustrated signals for help, is in no way creating a sense of structure. Structure is not a lesson plan. Structure is not dress codes, more suspensions, little slanted ticks in roll books, or rigidly imposed time limits on tests and assignments. Structure is not the pseudoscience of "objective" tests and numerical scores, and it is certainly not a tough principal. All of these things are symptoms of psychotic behavior in teachers, but none of them is structure. If structure exists, it exists in the minds of students and teachers; if structure exists in neither place, it cannot be brought on with rules and demands for more of it. And while these things no doubt provoke some kind of response in children, that response is more likely to be accommodation, acquiescence, and silent rejection than any kind of order.

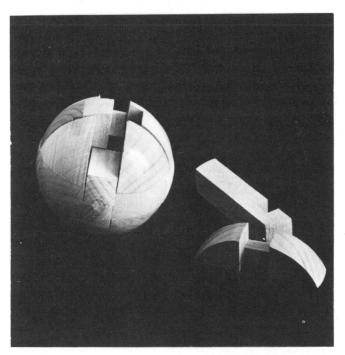

Structure is an internal thing, a state of mind, not imposed from the outside, but found, nurtured, and strengthened from within. Structure is something we feel inside. It feels good, and though we usually can't recognize it or are totally unconscious of it, we like it.

Kids know what structure is, and they like the kinds of things it frees them to do. Have you ever thought about the games kids play, games in which they enforce fun limitations *on themselves*, limitations which make the particular game work, like the spacial limitations of hopscotch, walking across a log, not stepping on cracks in the sidewalk, or the self-imposed silence of charades? Five squares is such a game, imposing strict rules of silence and giving, enforced by the teacher with a kind of benevolent sternness, a tongue-in-cheek autocracy that kids love because it has a purpose, a learning-structure purpose, and the rules are lifted once this purpose has been served.

As I said earlier, this very personal, internal nature of structure was, at first, puzzling. When I began putting this thing together I wasn't sure if it was even possible to describe structure, much less suggest ways in which it is acquired or imparted. But I have come to believe (at least during this moment in my life) that a sense of structure can be imparted, can be shared, that we can help kids use structured, orderly thinking—not to the exclusion of divergent, creative thought but as a means of freeing the mind for its real function: creating and being happy doing things. I think one of the best ways of doing this is through demonstration—again, not in an awkward, self-conscious manner. To this end I can offer models of teacher behavior which in turn help students discover order and structure on their own, and, at the same time, illustrate through example the kind of teaching that encourages a self-realized, internalized sense of structure.

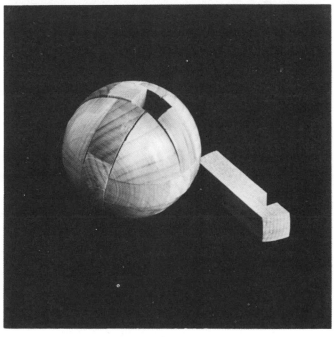

Implicit in the models and projects that follow is a sense of personal structure that, while serving as examples to students (and teachers), do not in any way impose structure as environment or program or impel students toward a predetermined line of action or a narrowly-defined objective. Students are free to find their own way (ultimately the only one that will work, anyway) within a context of shared ways which may be adopted, modified to fit personal needs and then adopted, or even rejected in favor of others discovered to be more effective and useful. These experiences can be carried off with confidence, humor, and respect for the different kinds of ways people learn to do things, all the different ways they borrow from others to build up their own learning, thinking, doing, creating strategies. Through them all is a sharing, a give and take, a beautiful rhythm that occurs not because we demand it but because we all feel it ourselves.

So now you know what I mean by structure as state of mind. It comes in all shapes and sizes, all schemes and patterns, and results in all modes of expression and creation. Structure as a state of mind is kids working on their own—but feeling secure enough to ask for help and knowing what kinds of questions to ask. Internal structure is moving through a series of steps in solving a problem or finding a way of doing something—making wooden masks of paper plates, paper shreads and glue, for example. It is testing ideas, building a flyable kite, planning an event, discovering how to use videotape and other media in a new context, developing a strategy for winning a game. A structured state of mind is making a mistake and then trying again, this time using your own ideas. It is being able to do things yourself, exercising initiative, trying out all kinds of ideas, finding a solution or discovering that there is no solution, being aware of lots of alternatives. But most important is the fact that structure comes from within, an expression of self-confidence, self-determination, and initiative. As nebulous a quality as it is, there's no mistaking its appearance. When a child has found it, there's no mystery, no hiding it. It bursts out with the intensity of life, with the purposefulness of a scientist, or a composer, or an inventor, or a poet, or a kid who's just discovered for himself . . .

Hey, wait a minute. I think I know a way!

IT'S CALLED
FIVE SQUARES...
AND YOU
CAN'T TALK!

Five Squares is a simple, uncomplicated game, which like so many of the simplest activities we do has a way of making magical things happen. It works well with all age groups—try it sometime at a department or faculty meeting—but it's more fun with kids because they're more real. I have no idea where or with whom the game originated, but I suspect that it's one of those now classic experiments, like putting pegs in holes or saying the first thing that comes to mind upon hearing the word "mother," conjured up by some behaviorist at the University of Michigan or somewhere like that to probe people's psyches, ids, and libidos. Anyway, it is something from the other world out there and not a device originally devised or intended for the classroom. It has not, in my experience, ever inadvertently exposed latent homosexuality, but should this happen when you play it just try to see it as "providing another dimension" to your teaching. Besides, if you're going to try some of the other things in this book such a discovery will probably happen anyway, and it's better to have it come out under "controlled" conditions! (Then you can always say it was part of your strategy all along.)

Like any good game or simulation Five Squares creates events which enable students to observe themselves and others within a group experience. The depth of such observations tends to be limited more by the teacher's hangups than any the students might have. If nothing else, the game has a socializing value. As a first day "mixer" it brings kids together into tight little groups, fuses them into a cooperative unit. It breaks up, for the moment at least, all those little alliances which tend to fragment the class, perpetuate themselves throughout the whole time that you are together, and make open, uninhibited discussion so damnably difficult. By gently coercing people to join a group you are helping them overcome the awkwardness of those first days and the inertia that makes it so hard to meet new people. You can make a part of the class those few kids who are always sitting out at the periphery, somehow excluded or excluding themselves from the action. Because it is a non-verbal game it can easily include students who don't speak English very well or, for that matter, who don't speak it at all.

This can be accomplished in other ways, however, like having everyone take off their clothes and tell where they were born and what junior high they attended—so you will want more reasons for playing Five Squares. Human behavior defies verbal description. The enormities, the subtleties, the infinite variations of human behavior can only be approximated—if that—by any abstract system of language. In spite of this, teachers spend a lot of time *talking* about behavior. This is further complicated by talking about behavior that has not even been observed, the behavior of someone somewhere else at some other time. Terms like "cooperation," "hostility," "conflict," and "self-centered" hardly begin to convey the realities of the concept they represent, and yet we continue to use these words in the abstract in an attempt to explain to students what causes certain social or cultural phenomena. We must begin by realizing that behavioral terms have no meaning whatsoever when used apart from an act or experience which can serve to give some meaning to the term in the student's mind and then, when repeated, can reinforce and increase the accuracy of that image. The Five Squares experience provides examples of behavioral realities; or, more to the point, it makes things happen here and now and out in the open so that we can see them and know them and understand how they work.

Five Squares then is an experience in observing behavior close up. As the groups go about their tasks many kinds of behavior appear, uncomplicated by language—anxiety, frustration, impatience, conflict, hostility, cooperation, indifference, interaction and isolation, withdrawal and aggression. Discussing these things is only incidentally an outcome of the game; more important is the understanding that comes through personal experience of what happens when individuals become part of groups.

Each one of us is asserting his individuality, sticking it out, saying "this is me." At some point, growing more frequent now as the world gets smaller, one's individuality "sticking out" bumps up against someone else's individuality "sticking out." What happens when a whole bunch of people all come together with their individualities sticking out, bumping, touching, sliding, abrading, carressing each other? It's called "society," and in microcosm it looks something like this . . .

[8:45] OK, the bell has rung . . . let's come down off the walls . . . pull your desks together into groups of five . . . right, so that they form a little table . . . [pandemonium, desks scraping across the floor, books, pencils, and gym shoes everywhere, loud talking, kids bumping and stumbling into each other—the usual comfortable, familiar classroom sounds] Not too close, let's keep the groups apart so you can't see what people in the other groups are doing . . .

Do we get to touch and hold hands in this game . . . like the last one?

I was just gettin' comfortable, man, how come I have to move?

You'll see, Sammy . . . trust me, it's Monday and we all need *lots* of trust if we're going to survive the morning. Now, I want to . . .

George, you look awfully lonely over there by yourself, join a group.

Do I have to?

There's a group of four over there who needs you.

Naw, I'm stayin' here, man, they don't need *me*.

Let's see . . . one, two, three . . . we have four groups of five, a group of four, and George. We're going to play a game today and it's called Five Squares, a really simple game that you play with pieces of cardboard, but to play you have to be absolutely quiet, no one can talk or make a sound while the game is going on . . . it's non-verbal . . .

Mr. W, you know I can't keep quiet that long, I'll bust!

Burst. Try, we all have to make sacrifices. Now, I've put the rules on the board and we'll read over them together to make sure everybody understands. Once the game's started you can't talk and I can't answer questions (see, I have to be quiet too!). First, here's what you have to do . . .

GROUP TASK

TO COMPLETE FIVE SQUARES SO THAT EACH PLAYER HAS A SQUARE THE SAME SIZE AS THE OTHER PLAYERS

In other words, everybody's got to end up with the same size square . . .

RULES

THE GAME MUST BE PLAYED IN COMPLETE SILENCE. NO TALKING. YOU MAY NOT POINT, GESTURE, OR SIGNAL OTHER PLAYERS WITH YOUR HANDS IN ANY WAY.

YOU MAY NOT TAKE A PIECE FROM ANOTHER PLAYER

YOU MAY NOT PLACE A PIECE IN ANOTHER PLAYER'S SQUARE

YOU MAY GIVE A PIECE TO ANOTHER PLAYER AND, WHEN YOU HAVE FINISHED COVER YOUR SQUARE WITH YOUR ENVELOPE.

It's a giving game. Now, you'll each get an envelope containing three pieces, but don't open it until I say to. This is a group task and you will be competing with other groups against the clock . . . any questions?

We didn't get any envelopes.

Hmmm . . . well, only groups of five can play this game, Ann, so I guess you're out . . . unless you can convince George over there to join you. All-right, remember, no talking and no fair taking pieces from another player. Just give. It's . . . 9:00; open your envelopes and begin.

[Students open and go through their envelopes, inspect each piece, and begin looking around at the other players. At first, each student tries to make a square from his own pieces, but it quickly becomes clear that he will need pieces from other players. How to get them is the problem. The group of four looks really forlorn; they're glancing at George, who sits alone, aware of their glances, looking very self-conscious and uncomfortable. Pieces are moving around the tables. It is a struggle to keep everybody quiet at first. With uncharacteristic sternness, I caution Bill and Robert against taking pieces from each other. Moving from group to group I can make my presence felt, increase the anxiety and frustration somewhat, and enjoy close up the squirming, furtive glances, and the contortions that bodies are put through in attempts at non-verbal communication.]

[9:07 Group 3 finishes. The players cover their squares, their faces reflecting triumph as they look around and realize that they are the first to finish.

Leona comes over from the group of four and whispers . . .]

We're bored just sitting over there. We want to play too. Can't you make George sit with us so we can play?

Why don't you go over and talk to him about it. Take him out into the hall and see what you can do. [Leona goes over and nudges George, who reluctantly follows her out into the hall].

Those of you who have completed your squares can get up and observe the others—quietly—if you like.

25

[9:15 Group 1 finishes. They get up and watch the agonies of the two remaining groups with smug satisfaction. Group 2 is at an impasse. The problem is that Loretta has a square that looks like this

and she has pieces belonging to two other players! She has covered her pieces, indicating that *she* is finished with the game, and is beginning to look bored with the others. She leaves her group, walks around a few minutes looking at the other players, and then comes over to me . . .]

Can I go to my locker? I have to get something.
Don't you think the group might need you?
No. I'm finished, and besides they're so slow. They just sit there.

[She leaves the room. Her place is now empty, her pieces (incorrectly arranged) are covered up. It is now 9:20 and two groups are still working. George and Ann have returned. George has moved his chair over and, still somewhat defiant but considerably more cooperative, sits with the group. I have given them envelopes and they are playing. The game continues with three groups—2, 4, and 5—still working.

There is a lot of animated gesturing, signs of impatience with fellow players. Frustrations are high in Group 2. Loretta's departure has left them helpless; she has still not returned and her group has all but given up. Three members of Group 4 have correct squares; the other two are shooting pieces back and forth, trying them out, and then exchanging again. At 9:30 Group 4 finishes with sighs of relief and released anxiety and tension. They are now the third group to finish and join the others, who have left Group 2 alone and are all watching Group 5. They seem happy to have finished, their humor and animated interaction contrasting with the dejection of Group 2, one member of which has now taken out a magazine and begun reading. Great activity in George's group, now. The five late starters are really working furiously, and for his part George looks contented and amused. At 9:36 they finish. George is bragging about bringing the thing to a successful end; he had the "Y" square which, for some reason, seems to be the most difficult to visualize and usually the last to be completed. Loretta returns and sits down; her group has disintegrated. 9:40 and the bell finishes the game. The class pours out in considerable excitement and comparing of notes. The members of Group 2 look stunned; they get up slowly with but a few words and walk out. They are the only group that did not finish.]

[8:45, the next day. If you have flexible scheduling it's better to have a discussion immediately after the last group has finished, as talk will be more spontaneous and feelings more immediate. But with some classes, like this one, the game is still very much on their minds when they enter class the next day . . .]

You got another game for us today Mister W? . . . That was fun . . . hey, how come Loretta left . . . I'll bet you're tryin' to psyche us out, huh, Mr. Weitzman? . . . I don't see what that has to do with social studies . . . Shhhhi, we didn't get a chance to finish . . . how come we did that? . . . man, that was really too simple . . .

It's supposed to be simple, Barry. Remember I said that it was a non-verbal game, a simple game? Well, because it was so simple, we had a chance to concentrate on the other things that were happening. Besides, words are tricky; it's not always easy to tell anything about people's attitudes, or intentions, or feelings about others from what they say. If we are too intent on listening and talking, we are distracted from looking at gestures, the looks on peoples, faces, their actions, or from really communicating with them. Words can, in a way, be insulators that do more to separate people than to bring them together. But before we say too much about what the game is supposed to be, let's find out about how it actually worked. What do you think this game was about . . .

Larry?

Well, it was a cooperation game . . . you know, because you couldn't talk to one another you had to really work together to get things done.

Mike?

. Like you said, it was a giving game. Like, I sat there for like ten minutes waiting for someone to give me a piece and then it hit me, everybody else is doin' the same thing, waiting for everyone else to give. Then I started moving my pieces around, hoping, well as sort of a signal to the others . . .

[Ann] You've got to think like the other person's thinking, you know, you got to think what they're thinking so you can know which piece they need and look to see if you got it . . . [George] I think it was just fun doin' it, I mean, you know, once I got into it I wasn't thinking about that intellectual shit, you know, I was enjoying playing the game . . .

Great. Now do you remember last week when we used the word "microcosm?" We talked about how a "microcosm" was a model or a kind of situation in miniature that, because it is so small, is easier to observe and talk about—do you think these groups of five had anything to do with that discussion . . .?

[George] Yeah, well our groups was kind of a small world, like there were all kinds of people in it . . .

What kind of people, George?

Well, you know people with all kinds of attitudes and feelings, like people who give and people who take, and helpful people, and people who don't help, and people who cheat . . .

[Mario] There are cooperative people and uncooperative people . . .

[Ann] Like Loretta, shhhii' you just got off and left . . .

Bill, and Catherine, and the others in Group 2, how do you feel about what happened in your group yesterday? How do you feel about Loretta? [I'm sitting with Loretta now, to attract and at the same time help her absorb some of the barbs coming her way. I think she feels better about it that way. I want her to face the consequences of her actions rather than just be defensive and ignore the others]

Oh, I don't know . . .

Come on Bill, what were you thinking when Loretta got up and left, was gone almost the whole period, and you were unable to finish . . . How'd that make you feel?

I guess I was angry . . . I guess . . .

She had no right to do that! We could have finished if she hadn't left.

Hey, Mister W, how come we couldn't finish with Loretta gone?

27

The game is designed so that although there are many ways of making squares, there is only one way to do it and you have all five squares the same size. Loretta's square had pieces in it that belonged to two other squares . . .

Yeah, we needed you Loretta and you took yourself right out of the room . . .

Well, I didn't know, and anyway you're all so slow. I didn't see any need to just sit around . . .

Loretta, didn't you feel any responsibility to the group? Didn't it occur to you as it did to Mike that other people were depending on you?

Well . . . what's the group to me anyway? They don't mean anything to me; they're just a bunch of people playing a game . . .

[At this, the class exploded. Loretta is not as callous as she sounds, but she is very independent and proud to a fault. Because she has a lot of initiative and an indomitable inner strength she feels she needs no one and thus cannot understand how anyone could possibly need her. After their initial reaction, the class became conciliatory, and Barry, who hadn't said much all day began to see something] . . .

That's really scary . . . that's, that's really bad . . You know, I've been there. But not just me, a lot of us here sometimes just don't give a shit about anybody else.

. . . It's really bad to hear it coming at you, I mean to see yourself reflected in somebody else's thoughts. Loretta isn't the only one, you know. When I was playing the game I was just thinking about myself. At first I tried real hard to make a square before anybody else did. I bet that if I had gotten my square I would have done the same thing . . . a lot of you would have, too, you just won't admit it . . . that's really terrible . . . we're all like that . . .

[We continued to explore the conflict between the individual and the group and some students began to talk about how they thought their self-centeredness and competitiveness was somehow part of their bringing up. Many felt that working together hadn't been stressed enough in school and in our society] . . .

[George] I think we need practice. You know, it sounds strange and all that, but I don't think we know how . . .

Then you think it's a good idea that I ask you to work in small groups a lot rather than working as individuals, by yourself all the time?

Yeah, the group is more efficient, in a way, with more of us working together on a problem.

But did you get more out of the group experience than just completing a task? After all, it wasn't a very important task . . . Loretta?

I feel like I know some people better in the class now. That young man over there, what's your name? Yeah, Raul, well I never talked to you and now that we've been sitting together I feel like I know you better.

George, what did you get out of the game, you really didn't want to play, did you?

It was all right. It was fun once I got into it. I . . .

[Leona] Why didn't you make him play with us from the start? You're the teacher, you should have told him to get himself over here and play with us.

How about that George, should I have done that?

Whooee he sure is a slow somethin' . . .

Well sometimes, you know, it just takes time. Sometimes you just have to ease into it. I'm careful, man, I just don't jump into everything. I may like it, and I may not. It's hard to tell . . .

How did you feel about Leona coming over to talk with you about playing? What did she do to you out in the hall anyway?

I didn't think it was none of her business what I did . . .

But you listened to what she had to say and decided to play . . .

[Leona] I still think that as the teacher you should have insisted that he play. That's what I would have done.

But, Leona, I respect George's right not to play. And I respect him for listening to you, and when he did decide to join the group, really chipping in and helping. I don't do everything I'm asked to do. There are lots of situations which make me feel uncomfortable and threatened. What would really be great is if we could talk about those things, like we are now, so that everybody understands how we feel.

[The class is really together now. Their reticence is gone, we've become very comfortable with one another. We're laughing a lot, caring a lot for others. I ask Leona and George to role-play the alternative situation in which Leona, as teacher, confronts George directly with his refusal to play. He becomes hostile and defiant in his role, forcing Leona to admit that even though my way isn't right, neither is hers. We're high on interaction, talking in a way we never have before. Greg is another student who keeps to himself, but he speaks up today . . .]

I liked the game.

Can you tell us more about what you liked?

I don't know, it was just good. I felt like other people were trying to help me. I mean, I was the last one to finish and I really felt like everybody was pulling for me, you know, giving me the right pieces and moving around to show me what to do. I had the right pieces but I just couldn't get them to fit. Finally, Bill moved a piece so that I could see how it went.

Why do you think he did that? It was against the rules.

I think he likes me . . . I think he wanted to help me.

[Later we talked about how it felt to be last, or not to have finished at all. Some of the students who are used to success in school and in life generally failed at the task, while others known as "failures" or "problems" were in the first group to complete their squares. I directed the questions to a very bright student who was last in her group to complete a square, and, in fact, had to be helped. I knew that this was one of the few times in her life a simple task had eluded her. It was important to me, particularly in a class of such diverse abilities and interests, to get this into the open]

Geraldine, you didn't do too well . . . How come?

I just couldn't get it together. It looked simple, but somehow I'm just not used to that kind of problem . . .

How do you feel . . . not in an intellectual way, but from inside?

Everybody was looking at me, waiting for me to finish. They were so impatient, like I was dumb or something . . . I was angry with myself, and I hated all of them for being so fast, so smart. I kept saying to myself "It really doesn't matter, it's just a silly old game, anyway."

Does that give you any insights into how others in the class must feel when they can't answer a question or do an assignment, can't 'get the pieces together?'

Yes . . . I can understand, I think it must be painful to be last all the time. It must hurt inside to not know and not be able to do what everybody else seems to be able to do so easily. That would hurt a lot. I think I would want to help someone like that . . .

The bell rang. No one jumped for the door. We sat there hoping that it didn't have to end, looking at one another. Slowly, everybody got up and left for their next class, not wanting to break the bonds that had grown between us.

Some other things that happened and we talked about:

Five Square sets, even for huge groups, can be made easily and cheaply from materials available in school. Paper squares will last five or ten classes; cardboard will survive an entire department, and plastic must be great to feel and touch and move around (although I've never gotten around to making plastic pieces). Squares may be of any size. I find that pieces cut from six or eight inch squares fit into 5" x 8" mailing envelopes. Students like to make them, so this is a good project for kids who like to do things and are looking for something to do in an art, engineering drawing, shop, or crafts class.

Here's how to sort the pieces into the envelopes . . .

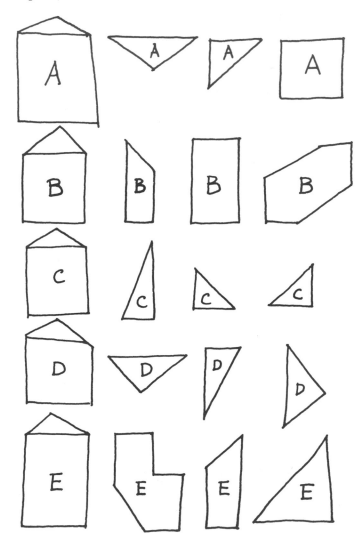

How you felt upon first joining the group; how you felt afterwards.

Did you cooperate with the others from the very beginning?

At what point did your attitude change?

Did you feel competitive with the others in your group?

Was your first thought "I'm going to be the first one to complete a square"?

What were your feelings when I said we were going to play a game?

How did you overcome not being able to talk? Did you use your eyes more, your hands, or what?

How do you feel about communicating with people non-verbally?

Did it bring you closer in some ways? Did it isolate you?

Did you feel angry or hostile toward other members of your group? What did you do about it? Why?

How did you feel about the group that finished first? (asked of those who finished last or didn't finish)

How is working in a group to complete a task different from working alone?

The letters on the pieces are there just to help you get them back into the right envelope at the end of the game, and sometimes to make the game more fun.

31

32

A Worker Reads History

Who built the seven gates of Thebes?
The books are filled with the names of kings.
Was it kings who hauled the craggy blocks of stone?
And Babylon, so many times destroyed,
Who built the city up each time? In which of Lima's
houses,
That city glittering with gold, lived those who built
it?
In the evening when the Chinese wall was finished
Where did the masons go? Imperial Rome
Is full of arcs of triumph. Who reared them up?
Over whom
Did the Caesars triumph? Byzantium lives in song,
Were all her dwellings palaces? And even in Atlantis
of
the legend
The night the sea rushed in,
The drowning men still bellowed for their slaves.

Young Alexander conquered India.
He alone?
Caesar beat the Gauls.
Was there not even a cook in his army?
Philip of Spain wept as his fleet
Was sunk and destroyed. Were there no other tears?
Frederick the Great triumphed in the Seven Years
War. Who
Triumphed with him?
Each page a victory,
At whose expense the victory ball?
Every ten years a great man,
Who paid the piper?

So many particulars.
So many questions.

Bertold Brecht

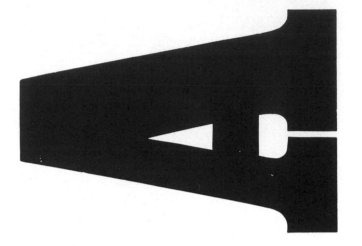

PLAY

PLAYFUL

Take a moment to consider your own personal image of an historic figure. Close your eyes. Now, let your mind form a picture, a composite of all the faces you have encountered on the pages of your school books. Your 'picture' is probably that of an adult male, older and quite serious. His dress is neat and formal, and it is more than likely that he is gray-headed, wrinkled and somehow faded. He is unsmiling, seemingly cold and unfeeling. The fact is that when we think of

people who have made important contributions to our culture, historically famous figures, we think of serious people. We tend to think, also, that the really important ideas and events of history were produced by mature minds, adults well-educated, determined, deliberate, and always thoughtful (look again at your picture; he has a furrowed brow and a look of intense thought about him). Of course, great inventions and ideas could only be the product of hard work. Teachers often complain to parents that students are not 'serious enough' about their work, or that in class 'their minds are elsewhere when they should be on their studies.'

Isn't it possible that someone with important ideas, someone creative, could be youthful, immature, maybe even awkward and careless? Is it possible that something important, something meaningful might occur in the midst of fun or play?

Just a thought . . .

Ludwig van Beethoven composed his first quartets at 15, and Blaise Pascal, who had completed a geometry book at age 16, invented the adding machine at 19. Alexander the Great was king of Macedonia when only 20 years old, and had conquered the world at 27. Benjamin Franklin was 20 when he set up his own newspaper, *The Pennsylvania Gazette*. Michelangelo sculptured his first great work at 17. When Wolfgang Amadeus Mozart was 4 he had begun writing musical compositions, and at the age of 6 was touring Europe as an accomplished pianist. Thomas A. Edison patented his first invention when only 21. Albert Einstein was 26 when he began work on his theory of space-time relativity. The Beatles launched a musical revolution when Paul was 20; John, 22; Ringo, 22; George, 19. Charles Darwin voyaged around the world on the *Beagle* at 22. Bernadette Devlin, from Northern Ireland, at 22 became the youngest woman ever elected to the House of Commons.

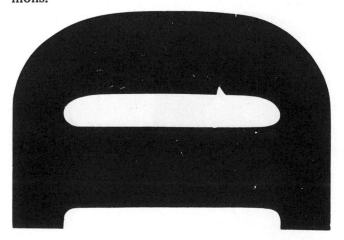

HOFFER

*Eric Hoffer has worked as a longshoreman loading
and unloading ships on San Francisco's waterfront
and spent part of his life as a migratory field worker.
Unschooled, Hoffer now spends his 'leisure' reading,
thinking, writing and talking with students. Hoffer
is a worker reading history and life, and concludes
that creativity is seldom the result of quiet, serious,
austere study. In fact, innovation is the by-product
of people in a playful mood . . .*

I have always felt that the world has lost much
by not preserving the small talk of its great men.
The little that has come down to us is marked by a
penetration and a directness not usually conspicuous
in formal discourse or writing; and one is immediately aware of its universality and timelessness. It
seems strange that men should so effortlessly attain
immortality in their playful moments. Certainly,
some have missed immortality as writers by not
writing as they talked. Clemenceau is a case in point.
His books make dull and difficult reading, yet he
could not open his mouth without saying something
memorable. The few scraps we have of his small
talk throw a more vivid light on the human situation
than do shelves of books on psychology, sociology,

and history. Toward the end of his life Clemenceau
is reported to have exclaimed: "What a shame that
I don't have three or four more years to live—I would
have rewritten my books for my cook." It is also
worth noting that the New Testament and the Lun
Yu are largely records of impromptu remarks and
sayings, and that Montaigne wrote as he spoke. ("I
speak to my paper as I speak to the first person I
meet.")

We are told that a great life is "thought of youth
wrought out in ripening years"; and it is perhaps
equally true that "great" thinking consists in the
working out of insights and ideas which come to
us in playful moments. Archimedes' bathtub and
Newton's apple suggest that momentous trains of
thought may have their inception in idle musing.
The original insight is most likely to come when elements stored in different compartments of the mind
drift into the open, jostle one another, and now and
then coalesce to form new combinations. It is doubtful whether a mind that is pinned down and cannot
drift elsewhere is capable of formulating new questions. It is true that the working out of ideas and
insights requires persistent hard thinking, and the
inspiration necessary for such a task is probably a
by-product of single-minded application. But the
sudden illumination and the flash of discovery are
not likely to materialize under pressure.

Men never philosophize or tinker more freely
than when they know that their speculation or tin-
kering leads to no weighty results. We are more
ready to try the untried when what we do is incon-
sequential. Hence the remarkable fact that many
inventions had their birth as toys. In the Occident
the first machines were mechanical toys, and such
crucial instruments as the telescope and microscope
were first conceived as playthings. Almost all civilizations display a singular ingenuity in toy making.
The Aztecs did not have the wheel, but some of their
animal toys had rollers for feet. It would not be
fanciful to assume that in the ancient Near East, too,
the wheel and the sail made their first appearance as
playthings. We are told that in one of the oldest
cemeteries in the world the skeletons showed that
the average age of the population at death was less
than twenty-five—and there is no reason to assume
that the place was particularly unhealthy. Thus the
chances are that the momentous discoveries and inventions of the Neolithic Age which made possible
the rise of civilization, and which formed the basis
of everyday life until yesterday, were made by childlike, playful people. It is not unlikely that the first

domesticated animals were children's pets. Planting and irrigating, too, were probably first attempted in the course of play. (A girl of five once advised me to plant hair on my bald head.) Even if it could be shown that a striking desiccation of climate preceded the first appearance of herdsmen and cultivators it would not prove that the conception of domestication was born of a crisis. The energies released by a crisis usually flow toward sheer application. Domestication could have been practiced as an amusement long before it found practical application. The crisis induced people to make use of things which amuse.

When we do find that a critical challenge has apparently evoked a marked creative response there is always the possibility that the response came not from people cornered by a challenge but from people who in an exuberance of energy went out in search of a challenge. It is highly doubtful whether people are capable of genuine creative responses when necessity takes them by the throat. The desperate struggle for existence is a static rather than a dynamic influence. The urgent search for the vitally necessary is likely to stop once we have found something that is more or less adequate, but the search for the superfluous has no end. Hence the fact that man's most unflagging and spectacular efforts were made not in search of necessities but of superfluities. It is worth remembering that the discovery of America was a by-product of the search for ginger, cloves, pepper, and cinnamon. The utilitarian device, even when it is an essential ingredient of our daily life, is most likely to have its ancestry in the nonutilitarian. The sepulchre, temple, and palace preceded the utilitarian house; ornament preceded clothing; work, particularly teamwork, derives from play. We are told that the bow was a musical instrument before it became a weapon, and some authorities believe that the subtle craft of fishing originated in a period when game was abundant—that it was the product not so much of grim necessity as of curiosity, speculation, and playfulness. We know that poetry preceded prose, and it may be that singing came before talking.

On the whole it seems to be true that the creative periods in history were buoyant and even frivolous. One thinks of the lightheartedness of Periclean Athens, the Renaissance, the Elizabethan Age, and the age of the Enlightenment. Mr. Nehru tells us that in India "during every period when her civilization bloomed, we find an intense joy in life and nature and a pleasure in the art of living." One suspects that much of the praise of seriousness comes from people who have a vital need for a facade of weight and dignity. La Rochefoucauld said of solemnity that it is "a mystery of the body invented to conceal the defects of the mind." The fits of deadly seriousness we know as mass movements, which come bearing a message of serious purpose and weighty ideals, are usually set in motion by sterile pedants possessed of a murderous hatred for festive creativeness. Such movements bring in their wake meagermindedness, fear, austerity, and sterile conformity. Hardly one of the world's great works in literature, art, music, and pure science was conceived and realized in the stern atmosphere of a mass movement. It is only when these movements have spent themselves, and their pattern of austere boredom begins to crack, and the despised present dares assert its claims to trivial joys, that the creative impulse begins to stir amidst the grayness and desolation.

Man shares his playfulness with other warm-blooded animals, with mammals and birds. Insects, reptiles, etc., do not play. Clearly, the division of the forms of life into those that can play and those that cannot is a significant one. Equally significant is the duration of the propensity to play. Mammals and birds play only when young, while man retains the propensity throughout life. My feeling is that the tendency to carry youthful characteristics into adult life, which renders man perpetually immature and unfinished, is at the root of his uniqueness in the universe, and is particularly pronounced in the creative individual. Youth has been called a perishable talent, but perhaps talent and originality are always aspects of youth, and the creative individual is an imperishable juvenile. When the Greeks said, "Whom the gods love die young" they probably meant, as Lord Sankey suggested, that those favored by the gods stay young till the day they die; young and playful.

LUHAN

Humor as a system of communications and as a probe of our environment—of what's really going on—affords us our most appealing anti-environmental tool. It does not deal in theory, but in immediate experience, and is often the best guide to changing perceptions. Older societies thrived on purely literary plots. They demanded story lines. Today's humor, on the contrary, has no story line—no sequence. It is usually a compressed overlay of stories.

"My education was of the most ordinary description, consisting of little more than the rudiments of reading, writing, and arithmetic at a common day school. My hours out of school were passed at home and in the streets." Michael Faraday, who had little mathematics and no formal schooling beyond the primary grades, is celebrated as an experimentor who discovered the induction of electricity. He was one of the great founders of modern physics. It is generally acknowledged that Faraday's ignorance of mathematics contributed to his inspiration, that it compelled him to develop a simple, nonmathematical concept when he looked for an explanation of his electrical and magnetic phenomena. Faraday had two qualities that more than made up for his lack of education: fantastic intuition and independence and originality of mind.

Professionalism is environmental. Amateurism is anti-environmental. Professionalism merges the individual into patterns of total environment. Amateurism seeks the development of the total awareness of the individual and the critical awareness of the groundrules of society. The amateur can afford to lose. The professional tends to classify and to specialize, to accept uncritically the groundrules of the environment. The groundrules provided by the mass response of his colleagues serve as a pervasive environment of which he is contendedly unaware. The "expert" is the man who stays put.

The youth of today are not permitted to approach the traditional heritage of mankind through the door of technological awareness. This only possible door for them is slammed in their faces by a rear-view-mirror society.

The young today live mythically and in depth. But they encounter instruction in situations organized by means of classified information—subjects are unrelated, they are visually conceived in terms of a blueprint. Many of our institutions suppress all the natural direct experience of youth, who respond with untaught delight to the poetry and the beauty of the new technological environment, the environment of popular culture. It could be their door to all past achievement if studied as an active (and not necessarily benign) force.

The student finds no means of involvement for himself and cannot discover how the educational scheme relates to his mythic world of electronically processed data and experience that his clear and direct responses report.

It is a matter of the greatest urgency that our educational institutions realize that we now have civil war among these environments created by media other than the printed word. The classroom is now in a vital struggle for survival with the immensely persuasive "outside" world created by new informational media. Education must shift from instruction, from imposing of stencils, to discovery—to probing and exploration and to the recognition of the language of forms.

The young today reject goals. They want roles—R-O-L-E-S. That is, total involvement. They do not want fragmented, specialized goals or jobs. We now experience simultaneously the dropout and the teach-in. The two forms are correlative. They belong together. The teach-in represents an attempt to shift education from instruction to discovery, from brainwashing students to brainwashing instructors. It is a big, dramatic reversal. Vietnam, as the

39

content of the teach-in, is a very small and perhaps misleading Red Herring. It really has little to do with the teach-in, as such, anymore than with the dropout.

The dropout represents a rejection of nineteenth-century technology as manifested in our educational establishments. The teach-in represents a creative effort, switching the educational process from package to discovery. As the audience becomes a participant in the total electric drama, the classroom can become a scene in which the audience performs an enormous amount of work.

My grandmother began school teaching quite young, at a time when it was still somewhat unusual for a girl to teach school. When my grandfather, who was also a teacher, came home from the Civil War, he married my grandmother and they went to college together. They also graduated together. She gave a graduation address in the morning and my grandfather, who gave one in the afternoon, was introduced as the husband of Mrs. Mead who spoke this morning.

She understood many things that are barely recognized in the wider educational world even today. For example, she realized that arithmetic is injurious to young minds and so, after I had learned my tables, she taught me algebra. She also understood the advantages of learning both inductively and deductively. On some days she gave me a set of plants to analyze; on others, she gave me a description and

sent me out to the woods and meadows to collect examples, say, of the "mint family." She thought that memorizing mere facts was not very important and that drill was stultifying. The result was that I was not well drilled in geography or spelling. But I learned to observe the world around me and to note what I saw—to observe flowers and children and baby chicks. She taught me to read for the sense of what I read and to enjoy learning.

Some years we went to school. Other years we stayed at home and Grandma taught us. That is one way of describing my schooling. Another way is to explain that between the ages of five and seventeen I spent two years in kindergarten, one year—but only half-days—in the fourth grade, and six years in in high school. If I had not very much wanted to go to school or if I had been a sickly child, probably I would have spent even less time in school.

It is curious that a family of teachers—for Mother, too, had taught before I was born—should have had such paradoxical views about schools. As a family we took an active interest in schools wherever we lived, and many of our frequent moves to a new place for the winter months were made with the expectation of finding a particular kind of school. However, my family deeply disapproved of any school that kept children chained to their desks, indoors, for long hours every day.

Kindergarten—the one I attended was a private kindergarten in the home of well-to-do people with a large house—was an expression of the most modern ideas about education. The training of eye and hand, learning about color and form and pattern by sewing with bright wools, cutting and pasting, and stringing brightly colored beads made of different materials, and singing in time to rhythmic play—these were all activities that my grandmother and mother and father regarded as good for children. Father appreciated the precision, the command over my fingers, and the ability to make things I learned in kindergarten: Grandma and Mother were more interested in the freedom to move. In their minds these two things went together. They were complementary, not contradictory—as is so often the case when one examines what underlies the more recent belief that children can be, simultaneously, spontaneous and obedient.

Looking back, my memories of learning precise skills, memorizing long stretches of poetry, and manipulating paper are interwoven with memories of running—running in the wind, running through meadows, and running along country roads—picking flowers, hunting for nuts, and weaving together old stories and new events into myths about a tree or a rock. And there were long intervals, too, that were filled with reading, reading as many hours a day as I could manage between playing outdoors and doing formal lessons. Of course, reading was a good thing, but too much reading was believed to be bad for a child. And so it became, in part, a secret pleasure I indulged in at night when I was supposed to be asleep or in the daytime hours I spent curled up in a hollow at the roots of a tree while I was supposed to be off on some more active quest.

From the time I was six, the question was not when does school open, but what, if anything, is to be done about school. We lived in a different house in a different place each year—first in Lansdowne, then in Philadelphia on the edge of Fairmont Park, near the zoo, in an apartment house managed by a distant relative of my grandmother's, then for two years in Swarthmore—one year "on the hill" where the college people lived and one year at the edge of town. The owner of that second house lived nearby in a smaller house, and we used to steal corn from his corncrib and feed it to his chickens. Prank-stealing was a part of life that was pickled in songs and stories, and we had to act it out. In all that time I had only one period of formal schooling—and then I was allowed to go to school for only half a day. I was envied by the other children, but the teacher was annoyed—and I was too, for I felt singled out and forced to be different. But that one year, the winter of my ninth birthday, gave me a clear idea of what school was like. Before that I had known only about kindergarten, a kind of school from which I had never wanted to come home. In the first month of that fourth-grade class I failed dismally in arithmetic. But by the third month I had worked my way up to 90 percent in arithmetic and had discovered that school was a system you had to learn about, just as you had to learn about each new house and garden and explore the possibilities of each new town.

Mother thought about every place we lived not only in terms of its schools, but also as a more or less promising source of "lessons." Whatever form such lessons took—drawing, painting, carving, modeling, or basketry—she thought of them as a supplement to formal education within the context of the most advanced educational theories. In Hammonton I had music lessons and also lessons in carving, because the only artist the town boasted was a skill-

ful wood-carver. In Swarthmore we were taught by an all-round manual training teacher under whose tutelage I even built a small loom. In Bucks County I had painting lessons from a local artist and later from an artist in New Hope. And one year Mother had a local carpenter teach Dick and me woodworking. She was completely eclectic about what we were taught in these lessons, provided the person who was teaching us was highly skilled.

Looking back, it seems to me that this way of organizing teaching and learning around special skills provided me with a model for the way I have always organized work, whether it has involved organizing a research team, a staff of assistants, or the available informants in a native village. In every case I try to find out what each person is good at doing and then I fit them together in a group that forms some kind of whole.

41

There are children playing in the street who could solve some of my top problems in

My House and My Family - watching out the window

physics because
they have modes
of sensory perception
that I lost long ago.

— *J. Robert Oppenheimer*

What To Do 'Till The Answer Comes

Asking questions to stimulate curiosity and the search for information, to help us find out things we want to know, is not only one of the most flexible and useful tools we have in the classroom but is also one of the principal means of imparting a sense of structure. I don't know whether question/answer sessions are the best way to get at a problem, and lately I'm leaning more and more toward group processes and brainstorming for problem solving, but I do know that being able to ask and answer questions is absolutely basic to any problem-solving strategy and that it is the most often used (and misused) classroom technique. Questioning strategies in various elegant forms have been the subject of countless articles in the literature of education over the past few years, all of which, good and bad, has served to focus attention on the way questions are generated and approached by teachers and students. Like all the other would-be sciences, the literature of questioning has created a whole new vocabulary for teachers, and so pervasive is this literature that I meet few teachers who do not know the right words; the problem is that I know even fewer teachers who can use the technique creatively. Nevertheless, the focus of our attention on problems of questioning and hierarchies of skills has had a definite effect on teaching, one which I consider all to the good. But I am concerned by three related outcomes of the events and discussions of recent years.

The first is that while teachers have definitely become more sophisticated in the knowledge of questioning strategies and, I think, are becoming better and better at formulating and presenting questions to their classes, students, on the other hand, have not become much better at answering.

My second concern is that if we look at questioning or, for that matter, any other techniques we use in the classroom, as models of behavior—and I consider everything we do to be just that—then I cannot see that students are getting any better at asking questions either. To the contrary, while all the talk about questioning strategies has made us conscious of the process, our awareness of what goes on in question/answer sessions remains at a very superficial level, and we've not even begun to understand the organization, structure, give-and-take dynamics that operate when students and teachers are learning to be better askers and answerers.

And finally I'm concerned about the inability of many teachers to live with ambiguity, to be comfortable with the reality that for many questions—often the most important and most interesting questions—there just aren't any neat, academic answers. I'm also concerned about their inability to be comfortable with free, open, speculative discussion which may, and probably should, take a turn away from the teacher's planned direction. While many teachers tell me that it is for the sake of the kids that they try to bring discussions to neat conclusions, it is in fact the teacher who is unable to avoid the compulsion to provide closure, to make sure that each kid leaves with a neat intellectual package at the end of the day. The small anxieties and tensions that inevitably result from working with open-ended problems which seem to defy definition, solution, and everything else, those tensions that stimulate further unconscious and conscious work on the problem, don't bother the kids as much as they do the teachers, who feel some kind of obligation to make it all come together. Let's begin with this one.

We must recognize that making answers the focus of an investigation jeopardizes, indeed precludes, any real problem solving. Focus and evaluation of alternatives are certainly crucial steps in testing hy-

potheses and in problem solving, but if emphasized too strongly too early in the investigation or brainstorming session they are fatal to the real exploration of alternatives and to creativity.

Divergent thinking, open-endedness, and free wheeling thought must be nurtured and protected at this and in later stages of the problem-solving chain. Yet the quest for very specific answers persists in classes, even though at times the problem itself hasn't even been really defined. I suspect that apart from any learning considerations, being able to write down or remember a piece of data or respond in a specific way is for many teachers, and thus for many students, a familiar act which gives some feeling of security, becomes a much sought after symbol of "accomplishment," a tangible sign of learning, and the only real evidence that something substantive has occurred. While all this may soothe and comfort, it ignores the tentativeness of "facts" and the importance of the underlying method or process of problem solving. But more of that later.

Another effect of having the "answer" is that it gives the teacher an unreal and unnatural advantage over the class. To know the answer at the point of

It is the teacher who is unable to avoid the compulsion to provide closure, to make sure that each kid leaves with a neat intellectual package at the end of the day.

*Another effect of having the "answer"
is that it gives the teacher an
unreal and unnatural ad-
vantage over the class.*

asking a question is a power few mortals have; to know the answer before asking the question makes the question irrelevant. Too many students are turned off to school simply because the only kind of questions and investigations allowed are those for which the teachers have, or think they have, the answers.

The work of social scientists involves them daily in a fascinating, intricate mystery. They cannot predict where their investigation will lead them, but they can be certain that once there, someone else, using equally valid methods and tempering each step with the same care and attention, will have reached an entirely different conclusion.

More serious than either of these is the specter of the kind of teaching that is misleading and unethical. Often what is called "inquiry" is nothing more than the process of allowing students to discuss a question, with the teacher then muffling or amplifying lines of thought planned to steer students toward a projected end-point to be reached. When the students reach this predetermined point, the teacher beams all over, is quick with praise, and tells the students that they have made a very important discovery.

It is this kind of manipulation that has raised growing and justifiable concern over the ethics of "inquiry" teaching. Having in mind an answer to the questions, the teacher unconsciously or consciously manipulates the individual students and the class in such a way as to make sure that each student and each class that day ends up with the same "correct" answer, while at the same time feeding the students' illusion that they themselves actually "discovered" the answer. This, of course, is unrealistic, because it teaches the student that the answer is always there, that someone always knows the answer, and because it leads to the same result as the constant use of the rhetorical question— an attitude of 'Why bother? The answer is coming in the next sentence.'

But even more serious is the unethical nature of this manipulation. We are leading students to believe that they are free to think, to explore widely divergent paths of inquiry, that they can really develop their own hypotheses and conclusions, when in actuality they are no freer and there is no more ambiguity allowed than in the conventional or didactic class. By the way, if you are really doing this, and your students discover that you are, you're in trouble. And well you should be. Not only have you destroyed your own credibility with the class—

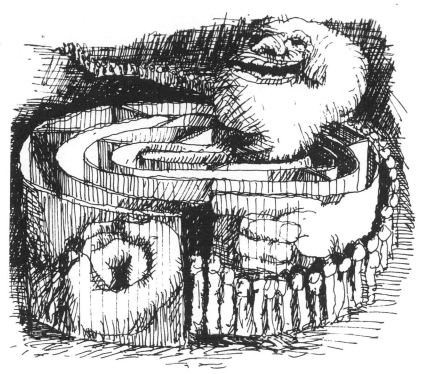

In actuality they are no freer and there is no more ambiguity allowed than in the conventional or didactic class.

an event one assumes would be of considerable personal concern—but you have once more reinforced a belief quite prevalent among most of our students: school is a shuck!

Another part of the problem lies in the tendency of most teachers to be answer-oriented, to be content with accepting the "right" answer, rewarding the student or students who come up with it and ignoring the steps which must be taken to reach the "right" answer. I think that it is better for a student to end up with the wrong answer yet know how he got there than for him to come up with answers that are the product of some really disorderly thought process which, though occasionally resulting in answers that are correct, totally escapes the awareness of the student.

While this statement may shock social studies teachers, my friends who teach mathematics and science understand where I'm coming from and take it in stride. For this reason, I need only go down the hall for an example of what I mean. When teaching children long division, or how to extract square roots, or balancing chemical equations, math and science teachers require that students "show their work," especially at the initial stages of learning a new operation. Confronted with a word problem in algebra, for example, the student must go through several steps including (1) reading and understanding the problem, (2) extracting the data presented in the problem, (3) determining what kind of operation is necessary to solve the problem, (4) choosing a formula that expresses that operation, (5) plugging values into the formula, and (6) performing the necessary mathematical steps to (7) arrive at the answer. Assuming for the moment that the answer is wrong but that the student has gone through the seven steps, the teacher need only look over the problem to determine at which point an error was made. Thus, if the student has chosen the wrong formula, the error is more serious and requires a different kind of help than if he had completed steps 1 through 5 correctly and then made a simple addition or subtraction error. (While I find one error more serious than the other, I will never forget being reminded by my high school math teachers that even though my error was "only" a simple error of addition, the bridge would still collapse and kill lots of people. Fearing that I would have to live with this kind of thing on my conscience, I decided at that point that math wasn't for me!)

Anyway, I think it is fairly obvious that this technique on a test or in a problem-solving session allows the teacher not only to diagnose exactly where the error is, particularly if it shows up consistently in similar kinds of problems, but also to determine specifically what kind of help is needed. The question is, then, can we use the same kind of "show your work" strategy in the social studies, English and similar kinds of courses? In answer to that question, I'll simply ask you to look over those seven steps above, seeing them not as just an analogy but as a model for the solving of a problem or the proof of a hypothesis in sociology, anthropology, history, or in any of the social sciences.

The focus, then, should be on what I would call "answering strategies," but with the understanding that the answer is in itself unimportant. The purpose of the question is not to get an answer but to stimulate and, if possible, look at the process through which the class and individual students go in response to the stimulus. The purpose of the answer, in turn, is not necessarily to provide information—although at the early stages in problem-solving we are interested in gathering and organizing data—but to provide check points along the way indicating the accuracy of the "work." In such a scheme the process of getting there is more important than that little bit of information you get once you're there. If you begin thinking about this it will do two things

to you. First, it will require that you re-shape your whole attitude toward questions and answers, which is good. Secondly, it will make you a lot more conscious of the kinds of questions you ask and the kinds of answers you will accept from students, and that's good too.

Perhaps another outcome of realizing the importance of the answering process will be losing your fear of silence, the silence that must necessarily separate a good, mind-bending question from an answer. If you stop to think about it, the most important things going on in your class might be happening during those moments of silence!

There is something else that needs to be said about answer-oriented lessons. Imagine yourself as a student who has not yet gotten it together, who doesn't have a structure or an answering strategy or whatever you want to call it. Sitting in class day after day, you hear questions and then answers, questions and answers, questions and answers—but you still know nothing of that mysterious process going on between the two events. Perhaps the teacher calls on you, and then after you fail to answer because you don't know how, she calls on someone else, who pops up with the right response. Then she turns to you once again with that look which says, "See how easy that was? Now, you can do that next time, can't you?" But you'll be goddamned if you can. You still don't know what happened; all you heard was a question and an answer and you have no idea how they relate (and they may not relate at all.)

Showing your work, then, also means making it public, exposing your mind and what goes on in it so that others can see how you're thinking and begin to grab on to some of those "mysterious tricks" that are nothing more than simple skills.

To illustrate more concretely what I mean by "answering strategies" let's examine the way children learn a simple mathematical operation like multiplication. Before you dismiss the analogy, let me point out that the mathematical example is more than just an expedient. While on a long tedious drive one day I began playing little mathematical games with two children, Peter and Kathy, both third graders who were learning their multiplication tables. Their method of learning was not much different from what mine was some thirty years before—writing and rewriting table after table until first the 2's are learned, and then the 3's and so on. One would expect that there must be some validity to this kind of learning, or it wouldn't have been

Showing your work also means making it public, exposing your mind and what goes on in it so that others can see how you're thinking and begin to grab on to some of those "mysterious tricks" that are nothing more than simple skills.

perpetuated for hundreds of years. Or would it? Anyway, Peter and Kathy had learned their "times tables" for the twos and threes that week, and to while away the time until we reached our destination in the mountains we each took turns asking and answering, 2 times 3, 4 times 3, 8 times 2, on and on. Then, at one point in the game, I asked Kathy how much 4 times 4 was. She looked puzzled for a moment. The usual rapidity and confidence with which she had responded to the earlier problems disappeared; she hesitated and finally explained:

"I haven't learned the fours table yet."

"I know you haven't," I reassured her, "but could you work it out or make a guess?"

Again puzzlement, a little inward struggle, and Kathy's answer, "No, I don't think I can; I just haven't learned the fours yet."

Meanwhile, I had observed Peter doing little ritualistic touchings of his fingers when he interrupted us and said, "Sixteen. Four times four is sixteen." Peter and Kathy were in the same class, and I knew he hadn't studied the table of fours either, so I was curious as to how he knew the answer.

"I added four fours," he said, "four and four and four and four, on my fingers, and got sixteen."

Whether his teacher had told him or he had picked it up intuitively, Peter is not sure, but somehow he learned something that many of us don't discover until we're adults—that multiplication is a fast form of addition. Kathy had memorized her tables well and hadn't missed any of the problems put to her from the tables of twos and threes. Peter, however, had learned a strategy. He realized that the product of 3 x 3 could be obtained by adding 3 to the product of 2 x 3, and that 4 x 3 was the product of 3 x 3 plus 3, and so on. When I asked him 4 times 4, he used a mathematical operation to find the answer, whereas Kathy was stumped, relying on memorization. Kathy's memory might fail (I still can't remember 7 x 8 and 9 x 8 sometimes), but the strategy that Peter had learned allowed him to work out his answer. This was illustrated again when I asked Kathy and Peter the product of 13 x 2 and 13 x 3 (remember, children learn the multiplication tables only to 12, and they had not yet learned to do multiplication with two numbers.) Kathy didn't know what to do after she got to 12 x 3; Peter simply added 3! By the way, Peter had discovered something of even greater significance, the theory behind multiplication on a slide rule (the addition of logarithms), a calculator (rapid mechanical addition), and the computer (lightning-fast electronic addition).

Peter and I let Kathy in on our simple secret, and now she can do it too. Faster than I can.

Now what does this have to do with us? Simply this: behind the most complex generalizing and synthesizing skills required in an elementary or secondary social studies class is a simple strategy, one which many students have not yet learned. While some may learn it intuitively like Peter, others will have to be told—if the teacher understands the process, that is. So often I have heard teachers praise the one or two students in each class who are so "brilliant" in their ability to answer questions requiring speculation, or in being able to generalize or to synthesize. Their voices reveal their amazement, for they themselves obviously don't realize that what such students know is nothing more mystical than Peter's discovery of multiplication as addition, and that any student can do it if we just let him in on the "secret" and give him an opportunity to try it out. The "secret" is a strategy, or problem-solving strategy, or whatever.

The analogy above was used because even in the social studies problem-solving strategies for elementary and secondary students can be reduced to terms of simple mathematical operations. Let's look for a moment at a typical kind of question that is unique to the history or social science class —the question that requires a student to determine the relationship of cause to effect in some event. For example:

What were some of the events that led to European exploration of the New World?

How did it happen that the industrial revolution occurred first in England?

What were the events leading up to and causing American involvement in Vietnam?

What allows some people to exercise social mobility while others cannot?

If we are to provide students with strategies for answering similar kinds of questions, we need to think in terms of answering or solution strategies rather than just questioning strategies. One way might be to consider this hypothesis: Causality is essentially a simple summation and accumulation of events. The key to removing this statement from the realm of the abstract and making it operational in the classroom is simply the recognition of the mathematical meaning of "summation," addition, which leads us to a formula of sorts that looks like this . . .

[event 1] + [event 2] + [event 3] + ... [event n] = the Industrial Revolution.

If we read = as led to, or caused, or resulted in, or brought about, then we can see that the events in this example might be exploration of the world outside of Europe and England, the development of mercantilism and trade, the publishing of Adam Smith's *Wealth of Nations*, the application of the principles of division of labor, the accumulation of "pools of labor" in the cities, and any number of events that might be identified as contributing to or leading to what eventually became known as the Industrial Revolution.

You're right, that's simple, absurdly simple. So why not let your students in on it? Consider the usual classroom discussion in which the teacher begins the data gathering stage by asking a question and then receives from various students bits and pieces of data like [event 5], or [event 10], or [event 3]. Then someone in the class decides to arrange them in chronological order or in some other useful way and finally comes up with the sought-after synthesis or generalization. That student knows how to add. While the other students know individual events, learned, perhaps, from the reading, or a film, television, a personal experience, or any of the other places we acquire information, they are not sure of what to do with them; they have the individual bits of data but not the formula to show them how to arrange and perform operations on the data. Their answer might be, like Kathy's, "I haven't learned my causality formula yet." Our responsibility is to teach them the "causality formula" and give them an answering strategy.

TO KNOW THE AN
SWER AT THE PO
INT OF ASKING A
QUESTION IS A PO
WER FEW MORT
ALS HAVE; TO KN

OW THE ANSWER BEFORE ASKING A QUESTION MAKES THE QUESTION IR RELEVANT.

act Fact Fact

Suppose, for example, a student wants to know the dates of the Shang dynasty. He need only check the chronological table found at the back of any one of many paper-bound histories such as Eberhard's *A History of China* to learn that the Shang emperors ruled from 1600 to 1028 B.C. Having learned that a good historian double-checks and confirms his findings, the student finds it a simple matter to turn to another book nearby on the shelf, perhaps Michael Sullivan's *A Short History of Chinese Art*, listing the dates as 1550 to 1030 B.C.; or to de Bary's *Sources of Chinese Tradition*, which gives 1300 to 1115 B.C.; or John King Fairbank's authoritative *East Asia, the Great Tradition* which shows the beginning date as 1766(?) and gives the reader a choice of two ending dates, 1122 or 1027.

Realizing that his error was in not following his first impulse, the student turns to the *Columbia Encyclopedia* to settle the issue and learns that the real dates are 1766 to 1122 B.C. or 1523 to 1027 B.C., the latter if he prefers the traditional chronology. If he then suspects that the problem is that something has been lost in translation, he can turn to Chinese historians Kuo Ping-chia, who accepts the traditional chronology (and after all he should know), Dun J. Li, who doesn't, or Chien Po-tsan, who takes the easiest (and most sane) way out, giving the dates as simply "16th to 11th centuries."

With so many "facts" of history so easily available to students elsewhere, why bother with them in class?

The acquiring of facts for the social or physical scientist, then, is not some end in itself. Rather it is another piece of data to be held up next to others, rejected if it is spurious and won't fit, accepted tentatively if there is a good chance it might fit, or accepted and put immediately into place, forming new patterns with other pieces of data. But each step begins anew the search for more information, more and more data, and increasingly more accurate generalizations and conclusions. Even with the "conclusion" the process does not stop, for this conclusion may, in turn, form but a small part of a much larger idea.

One of the frustrations faced by social science teachers and students is the incompleteness of the puzzle. Not only are some of the pieces missing, it is quite possible that they will never be found—perhaps because they are quite unknowable or no longer exist. At some point, then, we are going to be faced with making tentative conclusions based on what we have—an incomplete image with many pieces missing—the final conclusion, if there is such a thing, awaiting years or generations of investigation that will hopefully uncover what is not known. Finally, at some point, even with many of the pieces still missing, experience, reading, and even—no, particularly—imagination will fill in the unknown and allow the formulation of a still tentative but by now highly probable conclusion.

Teachers quick to give "definite" answers to students would do well to keep in mind that for the most part the puzzles worked on by social and physical scientists will lead on to answers that are "highly probable" and tentative, but seldom definitive. For some who still have not learned to live with ambiguity, the idea of all these unfinished puzzles lying about must be quite discomforting. But once we do get used to the idea, we realize that the tension of ambiguity serves as a stimulus to learn more and more about some of the old puzzles with pieces still missing and even to begin slowly and painstakingly to assemble the first few pieces of a new one.

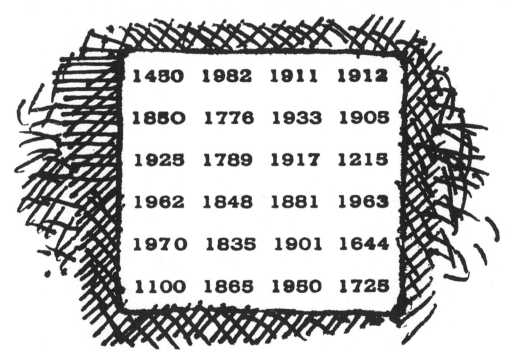

1480	1982	1911	1912
1850	1776	1933	1905
1925	1789	1917	1215
1962	1848	1881	1963
1970	1835	1901	1644
1100	1865	1950	1725

Dates. The pages of our history books are covered with them; but for what reason?

What should we do with them?

Memorize them? Read around them? Use them in some way?

Facts, we will have to admit, are useful. Without question, the acquiring of specific facts, even the most miniscule piece of data, is an essential part of some new learning or understanding. The most significant, most profound discoveries were often the direct result of what would seem to us an absurdly simple, even unimportant bit of data suddenly falling into place in some scheme of the creative mind. But facts have their place. They are the basic building blocks in a much larger process. Facts are not to be simply collected, like something that momentarily catches our fancy only to be put away without another thought. Neither are they to be acquisitively gathered up in a haphazard way, then left unorganized, undigested in any way. Facts are incipient ideas, bits of information which, like the myriads of dots forming the half-tone picture on this page, can suddenly coalesce into an image. Like the first stages in assembling one of those jig-saw puzzles of an abstract design, the work is very slow in the beginning as only a few of the pieces come together. But soon the pace begins to accel-erate as pieces, groups of pieces, and then whole sections come together. The image becomes clearer as more and more pieces find their place, until fi-nally it is all there.

So it is that individual facts have little value in themselves except to the extent that together with other bits of data they form a larger idea or concept.

That mess of dates on the preceding page, for example, has little form and purpose as it stands. But suppose we begin arranging them in different ways. One of the first things kids might do with a bunch of data is to group them together, organizing them into meaningful sets like

56

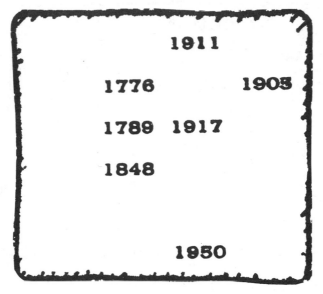

—revolutions

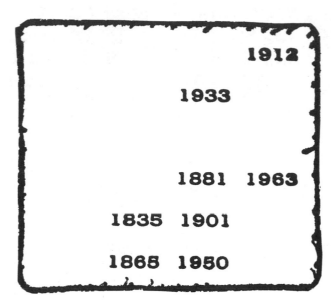

or assassination
attempts on the
lives of U.S.
presidents

Then, we might line them up . . . space them out
. . . and use them to answer a question, or test a
hypothesis, or check out a statement like one I read
the other day:

"Evidence of the growth of violence as an Ameri-can way of life is everywhere . . . in the recent pre-ference for assassination over the ballot in choosing
a President."

Is assassination a "recent" thing in America? Are
more Presidents being assassinated now than before?

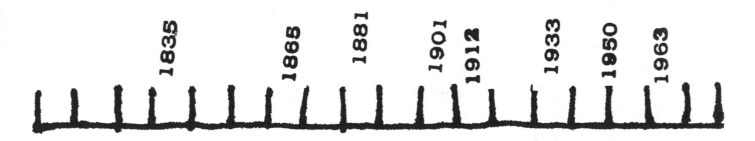

a thought: dates may not be as important as

the

spaces

between them!

Getting It All Together

The many ways in which creative people manipulate data and ideas are very subtle. They all but defy description and, so far, have eluded the grasp of even the most perceptive scholarly analysis. But creative use of information and ideas does occasionally happen, even, of all places, in the classroom—where important things aren't supposed to happen, only preparation for the "important" things to come. Occasionally kids just slip out of the confining student roles that are expected of them and become real users and masters of ideas rather than mere learners and digesters.

I can't define this when it happens, but I know it's real because I can feel it: kids of a mind, ideas moving back and forth in counterpoint, often during one of those informal moments like the talking that goes on just before the bell rings to start class.

Have you ever noticed that some of the most exciting things are said just before and just after class? It's a good sign, meaning that something's happening somewhere.

Well, anyway, one of those days just happened to end up on tape when a student brought her recorder to class as an experiment in alternatives to hand-written notes, and we were able to capture a few fleeting moments of what went on that day. I had asked the kids the day before to read some pretty scary eye-witness accounts of famine conditions in China, one by a missionary, Timothy Richard, written in the early part of the century; another by Theodore H. White, who had travelled through Honan province at the end of World War II; and the third a description of conditions in the cities. In the intense but informal talk that went on just before the bell rang I saw that students had been touched in some way by these accounts, and as I listened I realized that they were profoundly moved by a ghastly and pitiful human condition—one that is still occurring too often. Ignoring the bell and all the usual this-is-the-first-part-of-the-class-period-and-now-you-know-it-even-if-you-didn't-before ritual, I tried to pick up on all that energy, and we began to explore all kinds of things like the differences in historical sources, the uses of information, our own feelings and values, and something of the difficulties in trying to be straight about "facts" . . . .

Twenty million people in three years . . . starved to death . . . I'd have to be awfully hungry to eat tree bark and ground-up stones. It seems unreal that humans could degenerate to that . . . they're really nothing more than animals . . . . There's no mention of any government when all this was happening . . . I can't believe that there wasn't food somewhere for these people . . . I mean, surely people don't have to go through this . . . there must be enough food in the world!
. . . I wonder if it's like that today.

Weitzman: Well, I can tell that you've read the assignment for today. I'm interested in the things you are saying about the readings . . . Tim?

Tim: I have a question about one of the readings, the first one. It seems unreal and strange. Is it a real story? Is this a story or a novel or something like that?

Annie: It's from a diary.

Tim: What's the difference?

Martin: The missionary, Timothy Richard, actually saw these things happen; he was there. Every day he wrote down what he saw. I guess he carried a notebook or diary wherever he went.

Weitzman: Tim, what difference does this make?

Tim: Well, I guess if he's writing down what he sees day by day, it's probably more accurate than if he waits a few days or a few months and then tries to remember what he saw.
Martin: A diary is a more dependable source of information than a novel or memoirs or something like that, I would think.

Weitzman: Can you be more specific? I'm not sure the class quite understands. I see some puzzled looks.

Martin: Well . . . (hesitant, cannot answer).

Weitzman: Using the readings for today as an example.

Martin: Oh! Well, the first reading, the diary, seems to be more specific. He knows exactly which day he saw what, and even wrote down exactly where he was. The second reading was more general. He might have been there, but then he might have read these things somewhere else. I think a diary like this would be really important if we want to find out exactly where or when something happened.

Dell: The diary may be more accurate, but the reading "City Life" did more for me; it was more moving. The missionary seems kind of detached. But "City Life"—I can almost smell the crowds and feel the slime on the street. The first reading might be more accurate, but you can carry accuracy too far.

Martin: How can you be too accurate?

Dell: There's no such thing as accuracy when you're talking about death and filth and people in agony. How can you be objective about rotting flesh?

Brad: I'm with Dell. Look at the statistics given to us in the introduction . . . fifteen or twenty million people starving. Just what does that mean? Okay, how many people were there in China at this time, say in 1900?

Weitzman: Probably, four hundred to five hundred million. These are the figures given for the time of the Revolution of 1911.

Brad: Okay, now, if we're going to be "objective" I could say to you: well, fifteen or twenty million people; that's only five per cent of the population. Now, who's going to get excited about a mere five per cent?

Bill: That's Martin's point. Maybe, in the overall picture, five per cent isn't much, and you're . . . .

Brad: Come on! That's twenty million human beings you're talking about, not heads of lettuce.

Bill: See, you're getting emotional. You're letting the author cloud your ability to think coolly and rationally. I'd rather have the facts, and then decide for myself whether or not a given situation is good or bad. In my opinion, considering the number of people who are starving in the world today, I don't think twenty million or even a hundred million was "bad," particularly in Asia in the last century.

Chris: I've been listening to all this. I know something is wrong here, but I'm not sure.

Dell: What's wrong is that Bill is a sadist!

Chris: No. What's wrong is that you, [Brad, and Bill] are using standards .... It seems to me that some of us are judging events in China, things that happened a hundred years ago in another civilization, with today's standards.

Bill: There *should* be less starvation in the world today than there was a hundred years ago.

Chris: Right. In other words, we're getting all pushed out of shape over statistics which actually may not be as bad as they seem .... Today, in the United States, it would be horrible if even one percent of the population were starving to death.

Dell: It's happening!

Jennifer: That's another problem. But in China, in the nineteenth century or even in the twentieth century a loss of five percent of the population might have been unavoidable.

Serena: Even good.

Jennifer: Maybe that is actually a very low figure, considering things like population and corrupt government, or the primitive conditions.

Martin: What Jennifer and Chris are saying is that we may be applying twentieth-century American standards to an underdeveloped nation of peasants ... I don't ...

Dell: But, Martin, what other standards can we apply?

Annie: It doesn't seem to me that standards of what is or is not humane were any different a hundred years ago.

Tim: No, I disagree.

Martin: It's not a question of what is "humane" and what is not. It's a question of economics. Look, there wasn't enough food to go around, so some people had to starve; it's that simple! You're being sentimental ... this kind of thing goes on all the time, you know, survival of the fittest ....

Dell: Oh brother . . . !

Weitzman: Before we get off in another direction and Dell becomes convinced of our cruelty, I'm interested in pursuing her question of standards. Can someone suggest an alternative? Should we be conscious of the standards we apply to other cultures? Brad?

Brad: I think Chris came close to it a few minutes ago when she talked about looking at this thing from "different angles," or frames of reference, I think they're called.

Annie: And how are we to change our view?

Tim: Better yet, why should we change our view?

Chris: So that we don't get hung up on questions of what's moral or immoral, what's humane and what's inhumane, right and wrong, or good and bad.

Bill: We can talk about things more objectively, without our prejudices coming into the discussion . . .

Tim: That's impossible.

Weitzman: Why is it impossible, Tim?

Tim: Because . . . well . . . we are what we are. I can't look at statistics about twenty million people dying and say, "Ho hum, that's life." I can't believe people ever looked at death that way.

Martin: That's because you're not a nineteenth-century Chinese peasant.

Dell: Besides, you're not hungry!

Reggie: It still sounds like the world hundreds of years ago, before machines or anything . . .

Annie: That's just the point. Asia was terribly backward at a time when the United States and, I guess, Europe were more advanced.

Weitzman: Let me interrupt at this point for a moment, Annie. You're saying that all of Asia was "terribly backward" during this period . . . the late nineteenth and early twentieth centuries?

Annie: Well, yes, that's what I'm saying. It's the Asian condition.

Weitzman: Reggie, would you agree with Annie's statement?

Reggie: Uh, yeah. That's what I would've said.

Weitzman: Chris?

Chris: I think so. Whenever I think of Asia, I think of faceless masses, millions of impoverished, hungry peasants, meek, ignorant. They're all just "Asians" and I don't really distinguish between them.

Weitzman: Annie, how would you describe Asia geographically?

Annie: China ... Japan ... India, Vietnam, Korea ... Thailand, Burma ... Laos ...

Weitzman: That's a lot of territory and a lot of people. Can you really generalize about all of them?

Martin: Not Japan. She's made an error including Japan. When you first mentioned it, for some reason I wasn't even thinking of Japan as an Asian nation.

Weitzman: That's a rather revealing comment, Martin. Why is Japan separate in your mind?

Martin: I saw a program on TV describing the growth of the ship-building industry in Japan. Japan is now the largest ship-builder in the world. Considering the fight she gave us in the Second World War and now all this industry, I'd say Japan's industrial development began long before the Chinese.

Brad: Didn't Japan defeat the Russians sometime around the turn of the century?

Weitzman: In 1905. But why is that important?

Brad: As I remember, there was this fierce naval battle in which the Japanese navy really smashed the Russians, sinking most of the fleet. It doesn't seem to me that a backward, agricultural nation could have accomplished that.

Weitzman: What's the point of all this?

Dell: You don't make generalizations about things you know nothing about.

Weitzman: Precisely. But, let's not be too hard on Annie. Remember, most of you were willing to accept her generalization, broad and sweeping as it was, without question! In fact, I think many people would have agreed with Annie without giving it a second thought, and for the same reasons. Let's be careful about lumping people together under one generalization.

Dell: There's something else involved here too. Annie, I disagree with you on your description of China as backward. I don't think a nation is backward just because it's different and has different values.

Martin: Here we are at the question of values again.

65

Dell: To me, industrialization just makes a nation better prepared for war. Who needs the kind of "advanced" civilization of Germany or Japan in the 1930's? If this is being "advanced" . . .

Brad: I agree with you, Dell, but what Annie is trying to say is that economically China was well behind the United States and Europe. I don't think Annie's implying Chinese inferiority.

Dell: I think she was. It's an American reaction. Somehow, if a nation is not industrialized, it's not civilized . . . to Americans!

Jeff: We're missing the point here, I think. Industrialization, automobiles, refrigerators are not important in themselves: it's what they stand for. An industrialized nation has a better standard of living. People forget that if it weren't for our highly-developed economy we wouldn't be here in this classroom. Dell, you'd be knee-deep in mud and fertilizer, planting rice.

Brad: Maybe it . . . it seems to me that the Chinese never went through an industrial revolution . . . until today.

Weitzman: Brad has brought up an interesting point. It would appear that the Chinese did not experience the industrial revolution which occurred in Europe, then in the United States, and, later, in Japan. First, what leads us to this conclusion? If our conclusion is correct, why didn't the Chinese develop an industrialized economy? Brad?

Brad: First of all, they're still depending on mules and donkeys to do the work, and they're living in adobe huts. They're threshing and grinding hay by hand. In the West, in Europe and the United States anyway, work was being done by electricity, steam engines, internal combustion engines. According to White, few of these things existed in China as late as the 1940's . . .

Martin: He said also that transportation was as it was a thousand years ago.

Tim: There's a picture in the book showing men harnessed to a plow like animals.

Annie: Another thing, there's no mention of factory workers or factories in the descriptions of city life. Everyone seems to be a peddler, or beggar, or shopkeeper. It doesn't seem, from the reading, that anyone ever went to school except the upper class.

Weitzman: What does education have to do with it, Annie?

Annie: How can a man who can't read learn to operate a machine or work in a factory. Education must be one of the important steps in the industrialization of a nation.

Reggie: Why didn't they have schools?

James: Who had time to go to school? Even the children had to work in the fields just to grow enough food to stay alive.

Brad: Machines gave the Western farmers more free time and, besides, machines were more efficient ... it didn't pay to use children, so you could send them to school.

Reggie: But here we have laws requiring that parents send their kids to school. Why didn't the Chinese government do that?

Dell: Because, there are advantages to an ignorant population.

Weitzman: What do you mean by "advantages"?

Dell: Well, it seems to me that an ignorant population can be controlled more easily by the upper class. If the people had been educated they would have challenged the very special position of the ruling class ...

The major advances in civilization are processes that all but wreck the societies in which they occur.

—Alfred North Whitehead

BEHAVIORAL OBJECTIVES: SURVIVAL & GROWTH

Basic Skills

acquires, organizes, stores, and retrieves relevant data and concepts

learns how to learn and constantly improves on personal learning process

uses feedback mechanisms such as self-analysis to monitor and evaluate own behavior

determines, evaluates, and directs own destiny

increases mobility and flexibility without fear of disorientation

Personal Behavior

adapts to change without fear of losing identity, touch with reality, and personal values

develops increased tolerance for ambiguity

collaborates effectively in groups while maintaining individuality

anticipates change and makes adjustments in personal trajectory

willingly participates in the processes of social evolution and revolution

Interpersonal Behavior

understands inherent similarities and differences in all of humanity

enters easily into intense personal relationships without need for permanence, and learns to "let go"

moves freely in and out of groups

develops a large repertory of roles, feelings, values, attitudes, and relationships

adapts to and functions in widely diverse cultures and environments

identifies with and actively facilitates the integration of all elements of society

"I don't understand you," said Alice. "It's dreadfully confusing!"

"That's the effect of living backward," the Queen said kindly, "it always makes one a little giddy at first—"

"Living backward!" Alice repeated in great astonishment. "I never heard of such a thing!"

"—but there's one great advantage in it, that one's memory works both ways."

"I'm sure *mine* only works one way," Alice remarked. "I can't remember things before they happen."

"It's a poor sort of memory that only works backward," the Queen remarked.

"What sort of things do *you* remember best?" Alice ventured to ask.

"Oh, things that happen the week after next," the Queen replied in a careless tone.

Through the Looking Glass

We are all historians of a sort, pursuing and at the same time caught up in the flow of events from the past through the now and on to the future. In this same sense every subject taught in schools is a history course—math, literature, algebra, chemistry, crafts, geometry, art, English, engineering drawing, music, office practice, biology, cooking, physics, physical education—all are based upon principles, discoveries, practices, experiences, ideas, data, and even games accumulated in the past. Each is in a way a bridge between the past and the future, spanning Euclid and Buckminster Fuller, Bernoulli and von Braun, Voltaire and Vonnegut. This is, of course, as it should be.

But in schools it is not, for here the view of history is more than likely a record of things that have happened in the past and are somehow cut off from us—as Henry Adams has said "only a catalog of the forgotten"—an enormous body of facts which someone (we are seldom told who) has accumulated and arranged (for reasons which are never explained) in some kind of order (with a logic and significance long ago forgotten, perpetuated only in form.) It is certainly true that the historian, the scientist, the dramatist, and the mechanic are concerned with the past, but as Alice learned from the White Queen, it is an inadequate sort of history that remembers only what has happened and a poor sort of historian whose memory only works backwards.

History is not just a record of things that are, but a scenario of things, ideas, and institutions ceasing to be and about to become. The "past" is really a strange thing when you stop to think about it . . .

the past was once someone's future.

the past is a lot of presents and futures that have already happened.

the future is what will happen to us in the next ten minutes, but eleven minutes from now it will be the past.

People of the Middle Ages looking back at the "barbarians" considered themselves modern. We look back on them now and call them medieval.

Now we are modern, but
100 years from now, we will be looked upon as primitive
.... moving from the past to the future,
back and forth in almost imperceptible
steps, we will have to remember
what happened the year
after next.
The myth of the past is security and comfort. And the future is at once fascinating and terrifying—fascinating as long as it keeps its hypothetical distance and remains just a clever construct, an artistic creation, a futuristic movie or novel, a bit of Asimov or Bradbury, or an intellectual exercise. But faced with the ultimate reality of the future we become afraid, immobile. The future alternately attracts and repulses us in a kind of approach-avoidance behavior, so predictable, so human.

But these are abstractions, for we know this behavior in ourselves and others. Any of us who have worked on committees charged with responsibilities like planning a new school, designing a new curriculum, devising new scheduling patterns, or formulating future objectives and evaluation criteria recognize the pattern all too well. It seems to me that the metamorphosis of the group about to encounter the reality of future goes through several stages, beginning with . . .

1. Euphoria.

Assembled amidst all that seems so old and defunct, the new group is conscious of itself and its charge; there is an air of optimism and freshness. A sense of excitement characterizes the first meeting as brainstorming hurls the group from one visionary idea to the next, each feeding on, getting high on the energy generated by the others. There is talk of "finally getting out of the old rut," of "having a free hand, now, to do what we've all wanted to do," of "endless alternatives," "unlimited alternatives," of "new directions." The feeling is heady, exhilarating, like being able to breathe once again after nearly smothering. New trajectories appear; change is going to happen, for, after all, while we may not agree, we know what must be done.

And her face brightened up at the thought that she was now the right size for going through the little door into that lovely garden.

2. Reserved Optimism

It characterizes the next couple of meetings. A week of talk in the teachers' cafeteria, with students in classes, in the car on the way home, has generated even more ideas. But soon it is time to get "serious," and the fun, somehow, is over. It is time to be "realistic," to assign and choose specific tasks (for, of course there must be tasks.) The mood has changed as talk turns to projects that have a "realistic" chance of completion given the time and resources available. Perhaps the principal has arrived to caution the group against "moving ahead too fast," that is, moving ahead without exhausting all the possibilities for problems and hangups, without consulting all those that "should" be consulted, and without completing the necessary surveys and studies. The mood has changed, the excitement is gone, and there is a new tension in the air. The discussion, now sober and uninspired, works toward establishing priorities, making dates to meet with the bureaucracy, defining goals and objectives, deadlines, timetables for completion of reports, and ways of getting around the inevitable objections of conservatives on the faculty. All this soon becomes . . .

3. The Struggle with Impending Reality.

The group is slowing down, losing momentum. Two or three members remain enthusiastic, but they're isolated. Small talk and small thought prevail—who will take notes, is the committee properly balanced racially and sexually, what other members of the faculty or administration should be present, how will the work be assigned, what to do about the two members who have dropped out. The exuberance of stage 1 is gone now. When shall we meet? Haven't we gone a bit further than our charge? Shouldn't we call in the principal to reiterate what it is we are to do? Is it really within the education code to do the things we're talking about doing? Maybe it is someone else's responsibility, or perhaps they've already done it and we ought to "hook up" with them. At about this time the principal arrives and announces that the rest of the faculty is up-tight over the "politics" of the thing and that it will be necessary to clear all of the group's decisions with the entire faculty (and the vice principals, the superintendent's office, the school board, the fire chief, custodians, etc.) What happens then is . . .

> "The Dormouse is asleep again," said the Hatter, and he poured a little hot tea onto its nose.

4. Seduction by the Myth of the Past Occurs

Everyone is uncomfortable, wishing the stress and tension would somehow end, that things will return to "normal." The talk is defeatist. The problem is too big; no one can agree; a few people just can't make changes in such a large institution. Anyway, maybe we can continue on our own to think it out; no need to keep the meetings going (everybody's dropped out anyway.) Next summer would be a good time to get together and tackle the problem. Besides, the principal is afraid the discussions will "split" or "polarize" the faculty; bad feelings are beginning to appear . . . It's probably better if all of us work on our own, anyway. Besides, things are looking up, aren't they? The tension eases only somewhat, as the committee and the school acknowledge that they have been . . .

5. Crushed by the Insurmountability of the Future.

The group, its hopes, its energy, the momentum which seemed to impel it into the future, all chances for creating and changing, are stilled. The seduction by the myth of the past is complete.

The pattern is not only recognizable, it is predictable—so predictable, in fact, that administrators and faculties have learned to shunt off demands for change into special committees anticipating just such an outcome—inaction, indecision, terror in the face of change. Some groups disintegrate in a flash (I now bail out upon the appearance of the principal at stage 3) while others linger on in agony for the semester or the year, creating in some the hope that something will be done this time and instilling in others the confidence and comfort that nothing will be done, ever.

In the end the result is always the same. Those who might have developed new ideas fall victim to those who are afraid to; the lowest common denominator prevails.

But why does it happen this way? Why is it that when the need for change becomes inescapable, when action is imperative, when teachers and administrators finally seem to have recognized that the moment is crucial, when commitments and enthusiasm for change and new directions seem high, it all falls apart? There seems to be a very rational answer for such an irrational process, and it has to do with what happens when we get closer and closer to a real uncertainty (like the future), when we realize that we're no longer talking about change but are close, too damned close, to actually changing!

80

The resistance to change reaches its height and the seductiveness of the past becomes most alluring just as we are about to reach for, to actually touch and feel and taste the something new, the image in the distance from which there is no view backwards and—the worst of our fears—no return. I understand it all better when I read Donald Schon's explanation for such behavior in his book *Technology and Change* . . .

There is a conventional wisdom about the process of technological change. According to it, change is a passage from one stable state to another. At any given time, we are aware only of stability. By selective inattention and by making the signs of change taboo, we hide from ourselves the evidence of change. But when we look back, we can see that change has occurred. We seem then to reside in a new stable state and to look back on an old one, with a mysterious leap in between. This is a kind of quantum theory of change.

Under this general theory, technological change is a passage from one stable state to a better one and technology acts as an instrument for achieving certain constant social objectives. We see technological change, therefore, within a stable framework of objectives. These were well established by the eighteenth century, a century in which we began to see technology as the unquestioned instrument of social progress and to conceive what now may be called the Technological Program.

The loss of the myth of stability is frightening. It carries with it the fear of being in the Red Sea with no Promised Land in sight. Suddenly we are confronted with more information than we can handle. The job of objectives is to order and simplify experience by enabling us to select from it what will guide our actions. The dissolution of old objectives, coupled with a loss of the sense of a new stable state to turn to, is disorienting. Among the expressions of this fear and disorientation are the moral uneasiness and anxiety of our time, which express themselves in aimless violence, frenetic living and in a general sense of confusion and flux. How do we respond to these threats?

We can persist in the strategy of selective inattention to the changes going on. Change of objectives, and uncertainty associated with change, are as much *taboo* in our society as in the society of a corporation. We can give ritual adherence to the old objectives, systematically hiding from ourselves the ways in which they will no longer do.

But this strategy becomes progressively untenable as the evidence of the hollowness of the old objectives, and the inadequacy of the theory of the stable state, get borne in on us. Then we may indeed perceive the change of objectives and read it as deterioration. The call, then, is to Return. The appeal of the call is that it offers comfort in the face of chaos. There is change, but it represents a relaxation of standards, a loss of the good old objectives, a deviation from the ways of our ancestors, to which we are urged to return. The call to return gives rise to a form of sleepwalking, to use Arthur Koestler's term. Since the good society of the eighteenth-century program is, indeed, bankrupt, it cannot sustain us in the face of the problems and complexities we now face. The attempt to return to it, therefore, condemns us to a sleepwalking toward the future, of necessity leaving that future unexamined.

The call to Revolt has as much appeal as the call to Return. It is an alternate response to the destruction of the myth of stability. In effect, it says that the old objectives are hollow and inadequate. There is oppression, slavery, humiliation, constraint and injustice. There is no Promised Land in sight. Revolt against these things! The call to revolt need not produce its own image of a Promised Land. It takes its image from the present against which it reacts. It gets its concreteness from the life it refuses to accept and is, in this sense, a form of conservatism.

If we cannot be inattentive to change of objectives in our society and cannot accept the silent calls of return and revolt, what is left? How do we ever tolerate and stand up to change in objectives?

For a child becoming an adult, in revolt against the objectives of childhood and, characteristically,

of family, there is a need to seek out the next stable state and somehow in the process preserve a sense of self and self-worth. Typically there are individuals, and groups—peers, teachers, movements in society—with which a young person identifies. He is en route to their objectives. They are front-runners and he is catching up. As he learns the new objectives, he preserves his sense of self and self-worth through identification with these people. Front-running and catching-up make a pattern of change in objectives in society. But what happens, as at present, when at a fundamental level the society itself is in process of change in objectives and there are no front-runners at hand with whom to catch up?

When we are neither catching up nor in revolt, we can abandon objectives which were central for us only through an ethic governing the process of change itself. An ethic of change—which we may call a meta-ethic—provides discipline for the process of change, making possible abandonment of old positions without a loss of self. It permits us to tolerate the dizzying freedom and the surplus of information that come from abandoning old objectives.

A meta-ethic—an ethic for change, for inquiry, for discovery—permits us to enter the Red Sea when there is no Promised Land in sight.

The concept of an ethic of change very nearly appears as a contradiction in terms. Our norms are precisely norms for stability. We hold on to our norms and objectives, stand fast by them, keep them, and because we do, maintain a steady course which enables us to dispense with an ethic of change. Our moral heroes—Socrates excepted—are generally those who stand firm in the face of challenge: the martyrs to freedom and to God, the tough farmer willing to fight for what he believes in, the steadfast soldier, the faithful soul. We are apt to see change of objectives and norms, when it occurs, as inconstancy.

What mattered it to her just then that the rushes had begun to fade, and to lose all their scent and beauty, from the very moment that she picked them? Even real scented rushes, you know, last only a very little while—and these, being dream rushes, melted away almost like snow, as they lay in heaps at her feet —but Alice hardly noticed this, there were so many other curious things to think about.

Donald Schon's next concern, which cannot be separated from considerations of conventional wisdom and the myth of stability, is the question of what kind of a person is a change person. Schon's intention in this book, by the way, is to explore change in technology and industry, in the corporate world, but the principles are the same for teachers and schools and school districts, which undeniably have used corporate structure as a model (though they have managed to miss the point, adopting the most inefficient aspects of the corporate model of perhaps a hundred years ago and those which are least conducive to change) even to the extent of being "profit," "product," and incentive oriented. The problem is that the change-oriented person as presented in Schon's sketch is not likely to become a teacher and, conversely, people who are teaching are not likely to be change-valuing—suggesting that ways will have to be found to convert teachers who now operate under the assumptions of "conventional wisdom" or to create a new cadre of change specialists, beginning with selection in college, then through teacher training, student teaching or intern experience, and finally assignment. It is perhaps unintentional—though I think not—that Schon has provided us not only with a description and model of the "teacher-inventor" (to adopt corporate terms for the school again) but also with a set of objectives for their training . . .

And yet the problem of the development of an ethic of change now confronts individuals, organizations (companies and others) and our society as a whole. The individual asks, How shall I act when the foundations of my self (and the roots of my action) are disappearing? The company asks, How can we find our way into the future and maintain our integrity when it is no longer clear what business we are in, when the rate of technical and business change forces us to transform ourselves and the Great Man is gone? Our society asks, How are we to guide our course now that the instrument of technology has eroded our objectives and we are deprived of the illusion of a stable state toward which we are heading?

An ethic of change characterizes the process of change, as opposed to its product, just as the eighteenth-century objectives characterize the state of society. An ethic of change is a set of principles for change. A meta-ethic must, in order to be effective, have reality for us. It cannot be imposed artificially from outside. We must discover it in the very process of change.

In seeking a meta-ethic we suffer from the fact that society traditionally delegates the job of change to special individuals in its midst—to artists, poets, inventors, discoverers, therapists—and then isolates them from the rest of society in order to preserve the illusion of stability of norms and ob-

83

There was a short silence after this, and then the Knight went on again. "I'm a great hand at inventing things. Now, I dare say you noticed, the last time you picked me up, that I was looking rather thoughtful?"

"You *were* a little grave," said Alice.

"Well, just then I was inventing a new way of getting over a gate. Would you like to hear it?"

"Very much, indeed," Alice said politely.

jectives. Those concerned with change of norms and objectives, or with change known to lead to such change, live in well-insulated social compartments. Inventors, discoverers and artists live apart by a convenient division of labor which enables the rest of society to maintain an illusion of stability. Society allows their products to enter, hemmed in by suitable resistances, but protects itself from their processes. The garret, the laboratory, the studio, the closed study and the hospital are the symbols of this isolation.

Because of the isolation of those concerned with the process of change, we still find change of norm and objective mysterious. We lack models to help us now that we are, as a whole, beginning to experience the need for a meta-ethic not as individuals only but as a society. The need for discovery of norms and objectives forced by technological change and its consequences finds us without norms for this process of discovery.

At this point, we return to the subject matter with which this book began; the process of invention. But we return to it now for what it has to teach us about invention of norms and objectives. We cannot assume that inventors—or artists, discoverers and therapists—can help us directly with the generation of a meta-ethic. These men insulate the parts of their lives in which they are principally concerned with change and may be conservatives in all parts of their lives not directly related to their occupations. Nevertheless, the relevant parts of their lives as discoverers reveal aspects of change in norms and objectives. Some of the more important, in the present context, are these:

the prizing of the process of discovery itself;
the prizing of the here-and-now and with it the imperative, Start from where you are!;
the priority of experiment;
the projective use of the past.

The inventor becomes, in a sense, addicted to the process of discovery itself. He is excited by the new, *his* new; he finds tiresome the continuing presentation of what has been done. He has vivid in his imagination the sense of new energy and vitality that comes with insight and that has the quality of opening up and revealing new views together with a sense of power for exploring them. The inventor develops a taste for this experience. It breaks in on what is supposed to be or what may be supposed to be routine and well ordered. This love of the experience of uncovering something hidden before—an experience associated with delight and heightened energy—links the process of discovery and invention to processes of artistic creation and discovery. In all such instances, the search for the new—the new "for me"—becomes controlling.

84

"I'll tell you how I came to think of it," said the Knight. "You see, I said to myself, 'The only difficulty is with the feet; the *head* is high enough already.' Now, first I put my head on top of the gate—then the head's high enough; then I stand on my head—then the feet are high enough, you see; then I'm over, you see."

Discovery demands contact with reality—with the way things are. It demands starting from where, in fact, you are—not where you thought you were. It demands attention to what is happening now. It requires priority for the here and now. This is the priority of immediate experience.

For the most part we perceive in terms of the past and in abstractions. We see *through* concepts. We see objects. We rarely see just *this* now. And if we do, we are quick to turn it into a familiar object. But the process of invention has in it a phenomenology that is different. It is a matter of turning to the process going on now. Vonnegut examining his ice crystals and droplets. Walton attentive to what happens to the paper as it is deformed, the old mechanic looking and feeling the metal as it bends, pay a very special sort of attention to what is given to them. This kind of attention has in it something very much like what people have talked about as aesthetic experience, and it is as necessary to invention as it is to aesthetic activity.

As far as I am concerned, I experience a kind of terror as I am about to go to work and before the infinite possibilities offered to me, I feel that everything is permitted. If everything is permitted, best and worst, if nothing offers any resistance every effort is inconceivable. I can't base myself on anything and from then on every enterprise is in vain...

Nevertheless, I will not perish. I will conquer my terror and will take assurance from the notion that I have the seven notes of the scale in its chromatic intervals, its strong or weak beats are within my reach, and that I hold in this way solid and concrete elements which offer me as vast a field of experiment as this vague and vertiginous incident which has just frightened me . . . . What pulls me out of the anguish caused by unconditional freedom is that I always have the faculty of concentration on the concrete things which are in question here and now. —Igor Stravinsky, 1945.

The inventor's or artist's here-and-now takes priority in another sense as well: it is the priority of what *he* saw, felt or experienced as against what others say or believe. It allows him to champion his findings against the entrenched opposition of others. Similarly, the priority of the here-and-now of feelings and of interpersonal happenings—"what is going on between you and me now"—gives the therapist the basis for *his* discoveries against the abstractions and permits him to pit these discoveries against the abstractions and sense of the past brought to the situation by the patient.

For the inventor the need to test, and to create situations in which testing is possible, follows from the priority of the process of discovery. The priority given to experiment reflects both the need to

85

see "what would happen if . . ." and unwillingness to accept the content of feelings or intuitions without test. It reflects both the disposition to explore and a toughness about what will be accepted.

From the first point of view, the experimental attitude says that when confronted with uncertainty, you try things rather than fall back on accepted beliefs, on authority, or lapse into inaction. You try new approaches and, rather than accept plausible-sounding hypotheses, you ask how they can be tested, and test them. If there is no way in which they can be tested, you lose interest in them.

The priority of experiment implies a discipline. Testing is impossible unless there are rules of inference for inferring the consequences of a belief, methods of measurement to determine the consequences of action, and controls during the period of testing.

The inventor has a special way of using the past. In most of our lives we use the past literally. That is, we look at the present situation as an instance of rules and concepts that have been learned. Thus we are always seeing "trees," "animals," "business" and "entertainment"—concepts with which we are familiar. This is precisely what precludes the possibility of invention or discovery. The inventor, with his preoccupation with the here-and-now, tends to use the past in another way: to exploit the past as a basis for analogies, to use familiar theory as a pro-

jective model for present situations. This is what I have called in another context, "Displacement of Concepts." We saw in Chapter I how technologies, disciplines, methods and theories become projective models for what is unfamiliar and troublesome in the present situation. This attitude toward the uses of the past is precisely opposite to the attitudes toward the past implicit in the strategies of "return" and "revolt," both of which require that the principles and theories of the past be taken literally in their application to the present.

The priority of the process of discovery, the here-and-now, experiment and the projective use of the past underlie norms for the process of invention.

Children growing up today face a future without a Promised Land. If they are to develop a sense of themselves and of their own worth, they will have to develop an ethic of change. They will have to accept, as continuing, the changes in technology, institutions and objectives which have outmoded the Technological Program; they will have to identify themselves instead as those who trust themselves to the here-and-now, who start from where they are, who experiment, who seek the metaphors for the future inherent in their traditions, who permit freedom to change, seek new visions and become.

Donald Schon

Alice looked round her in great surprise. "Why, I do believe we've been under this tree the whole time! Everything's just as it was!"

"Of course it is," said the Queen. "What would you have it?"

"Well, in *our* country," said Alice, still panting a little, "you'd generally get to somewhere else—if you ran very fast for a long time, as we've been doing."

"A slow sort of country!" said the Queen. "Now, *here*, you see, it takes all the running *you* can do to keep in the same place. If you want to get somewhere else, you must run at least twice as fast as that!"

MR COOL MEETS

Bob Falk has been teaching about four years now, but he's obviously spent a bigger part of his life than that thinking about institutions, teachers, kids, and what goes on in, around, and between them. In this short career Bob has learned more about the most elemental, the most essential processes of thinking and problem-solving than anyone I know. When I first met him he was, like many of us in our first and most insecure years of teaching, deep into his subject-thing which, for him, was government and American politics. But even in his first semester "Bob the political scientist" was critical of the passivity, the impersonal blandness of textbooks and the closed, tight spaces they create, and I can still remember some of the ingenious simulations and brainstorming activities he generated with his kids that first year. Nor will I ever forget the semester that the two of us collaborated on a project so effective and so popular with kids that for months after, every riot, fire, and lunchroom melee was immediately attributed to us by the principal. Since those days of infamy we have both mellowed somewhat, and were this a different kind of book we'd be happy to share some of those early "projects" with you. But this is a different kind of book, Bob is now a very different kind of teacher than he was then. So when we sat down over wine, cheese, and tape Bob began with what he had discovered about the importance of language, where this all took him, and how he got from there to here . . .

PIERO DI COSIMO

The last time I saw you, you said you were doing something different, that you had decided you were going to teach reading. What I want to talk about first is the genesis of that revelation, the sudden idea that you were going to be doing something different. In other words, you're different this fall, and certainly different these past couple of years, than when you were student teaching.

I'm different each fall, but different in a different way. This year's revelation—it probably occurred much earlier, but I wasn't sure what to do about it—is simply that you can't teach social studies to people who can't read.

You're talking about basic vocabulary now . . .

Yes, basic words, even simple connectives. You know those incredibly long sentences we get, glued together with a dozen or more "and's." How many of our students understand the exact function of words like "therefore," "however," . . . even "but"?

It's customary to blame the English department, who in turn blame the junior high school English teachers, and on and on . . .

Exactly. This kind of analysis lets everyone off the hook, because you know you can't change home and society, and that's where the fault lies. But in this case I had the power to do something, and the decision wasn't hard to make. I could abandon the text, abandon the kids, or teach them how to read the text. By abandon the text, I mean not use a text.

What do you mean by "abandon the kids"?

Continue to assign them chapters they can't

read, administer tests they can't pass, pretend they haven't tried, fail a large number of students . . . in both senses. Or adjust the grading scales so that everyone who makes an effort passes, which is probably worse.

So how, then, are you teaching reading in your American Problems classes?

I'll skip the evolution, including some false starts . . . Simply, they begin by helping themselves. I urge students to work together. I urge friends to shove their desks together during study periods. I'll often say to a student who asks me for help, "Why don't you ask so-and so? She got a perfect score on the last three quizzes. She really knows these words." I work with students too, of course, but the cultural and generational gaps, the language barrier that exists between my students and the people who write dictionaries . . . it exists between me and my students too. Usually it doesn't matter that much . . . we communicate.

So far we've been talking mainly about vocabulary. What other kinds of skills do you see being emphasized within a social studies framework?

Observing, describing, comparing, inferring. Some of these obviously depend on knowing the conventional labels we assigned to concepts. For example, you can hardly describe an event if you don't know the names of its parts. But other skills also depend—sometimes not so obviously—on word-symbols. I'm just beginning to realize the extent to which vocabulary influences thought processes. Of course I don't mean passive vocabulary. What we call intelligence requires both a supply of experiences and the mental machinery to organize those experiences. But this is only potential intelligence. Intelligent *behavior*, which is the sign of developed intelligence, requires the ability to manipulate word-symbols. I'm simply pointing out that you can't do much with a concept until you know its name.

I've thought of things I've been doing recently as being old-fashioned. I'm doing a workbook, for example, and I know that workbooks have had a bad name for a long time. There was a study done recently that tracked down the 32 most important educational innovations in the last 10 years; it had a way of quantifying the survival rate of the innovations—teaching machines, team learning, team teaching—and the survival rate is very low. I'm not worried very much about being old-fashioned any more. I used to be. I feel that the way I'm using worksheets and workbooks is new-fangled rather than old-fashioned. I have a student teacher who saw some of my sheets and picked them up without any suggestion on my part. He kind of worshipped the idea, where I respect it, so I know that in at least one case it's very easy to implement. I don't believe very much in formula, really, for teaching.

But certainly, in a way, change has become very much a formula with you. . .

What I really dread, and what I think any teacher ought to dread, is coming to a point where you are not changing. I don't mean to suggest that change per se is good. It's just that I do believe that all people are either stagnant or slowly improving, and in the process of improving you make mistakes, of course, and you erase, erase. But I think on the whole—every day, in every way—those of us who are alive are getting better and better.

Change is scary to a lot of people, and you and I have talked about the ways this fear shows up in the behavior of our own faculty. It seems to me that what is scary is admitting to one's self that the old way is no longer effective. It's not that the new way is so threatening, but there's that feeling inside that to change somehow means that the old way was wrong and that other people will interpret it that way, will interpret it as failure, or worse, some kind of instability of character, or inconsistency. We're so goddamned afraid of being wrong . . .

As soon as I made the change, I realized that there had been nagging doubts all along, and this is the closest thing in my teaching career to what could be called a crisis. Sometimes I suspect that there are other nagging doubts too. . . . You know, I don't see it as having quite that much of a road-to-Damascus flavor, nor do I mean that it was the one time in my teaching career when I'd been wrong, but to me it's just been the most important discovery. Well, it has to do with some very strong feelings I have about language. Maybe that ought to be covered just a little . . .

Your concept of "the unity of knowledge" intrigues me because it tends to support one of my ideas, the need to break down the artificial lines of separation between "subject areas." There is no such thing, really, as a "subject" in high school, certainly not in the discrete categories in which we place them now . . .

I'm very interested in thought processes right now, and I guess I'm in the process of formulating my first theory of education, which I'll probably call unity of knowledge when I'm through formulating it. I do see certain rather elementary mental processes that run through every subject that's taught in high school, and almost in every compartment of life. To educated adults they seem obvious, perhaps to most middle-class junior high school students they would seem obvious; but we're dealing with a lot of students, many of them entitled to vote now, who don't understand these very elementary processes that have to do with seeing simple categories—for example, cause and effect relationships.

By compartmentalizing knowledge in the schools we've perpetuated this whole language problem. A social studies teacher will use the term "society," a math teacher will speak of a "set," a biology teacher will talk about "species," an English teacher may talk about groups of words, nouns or verbs. The need for a common, basic language suggests itself. And yet, you know how teachers are; you know the politics of teachers. You don't dare infuriate colleagues, even at the local level, by calling a conference to work out a common language as applied to common phenomena in concepts. If someone had the courage to do so, it might work. Maybe there wouldn't be any problem, but we'd have to rewrite all the textbooks and watch ourselves very closely when we speak to students. If you ask someone what is the one single skill that an education ought to give to a student, the answer of course would be "how to think." And yet thinking is the one department, the one class that is not instituted in American high schools, nor in junior high schools or elementary schools. We assume the students make inferences which in fact they do not make; we assume a lot about lateral transfer, which I think is indefensible. We assume that every child can distinguish printed letters from white background, but it is known now that they can't, even when there's no visual impairment whatever.

But I think you've picked a hard row to hoe for other reasons, you're asking people to give up positions of privilege. What you're asking is that we go back to being all-day elementary school teachers, and you know what the status of elementary school teachers is as seen through the eyes of others. What I would ask teachers to do is simply to be real and human and to understand that the natural world, the real world, is not structured the way a school is structured and that the school ought to reflect the real world.

I know that the change is not going to come from teachers as a body, nor from administrators;

certainly not from the community. I think it's too
trivial a matter for God to come down out of heaven, and so I think it will happen only through evolution. Someone said once that education is the
most passive force for change of all, second only
to prayer. Once I brought myself to agree, I had
to live with that reality. All right, we've thrown
out an idea and certainly we're not the first ones
to do it. I do believe in the slow perfectibility of
man over the course of the centuries.

I'll tell you a story about a guy named Zack, who
is trying to turn his life around. But he probably
won't . . . can't. He hasn't been well educated,
though he probably has more potential than most
of us. I call him Mr. Cool to myself, because whenever I talk to him he usually answers "I can dig it,"
"I hear you talkin'," "Right on," . . . that kind of
response. Or maybe he'll just wave his hand slowly
across the empty space between us.

But he doesn't seem comfortable in that role.
He can't sustain that role. What happens is Zack
gets agitated by certain ideas that come up in class
and tries to give long speeches. He can't, though,
because he doesn't know many words. So he mixes
a lot of malapropisms and near-words in with the
few words he knows.
Soon people begin to laugh at Zack, so Zack goes
back into his shell. But only for a few days. Zack
always comes back. He keeps laying his ego on the
line. He wants that badly to be understood.

Then last week I showed a slide of an allegorical
painting called *The Discovery of Honey*. It was
done around 1500 by Piero di Cosimo, a rather unusual artist. At least one critic thinks it represents
the transition from a nomadic to an agricultural
way of life. But the fact that it's ambiguous, and
a very busy painting, makes it ideal for practicing
the kinds of skills we were talking about a few
minutes ago.

A few kids did a fair job of describing the painting, but no one tried to interpret it. So I gave up
and told them the title. And that was when Zack
took off. I could decode just enough of what he
was saying to understand that he saw the tree in
the center of the painting as representing the way
to progress, that climbing it stood for aspiration,
that the particular event was merely an example, a
symbol, a suggestion, a depiction of the myriad
joys of *all* the discoveries men have made across
time and space . . . and that we were all literal-
minded fools. The more people around him snick-
ered, the more he sputtered, but this time he would

93

not stop. Even in that dim room you could see the anger and frustration on his face, you could hear it in his voice. Finally I said, "I know exactly what you mean, and I agree." That seemed to end the matter.

But it's been five days now, and Zack hasn't said a word. I guess that's being *super* cool. Someone should have told him a long time ago that he had ideas worth listening to, and then he might have taken the trouble to learn the names of some of those complex notions swelling up inside his brain.

Bob Falk's "workbook" is probably not what you imagine it to be; I suppose "workbook" is a term that for many of us has been ruined forever. You need to visit his class as I did—and Bob would certainly welcome you—to see the Falk workbook in action. No sooner had the bell rung, than Bob was passing out little wooden blocks (about ½" x 2" x 6"), six to a student, and a leaf from Falk's Fascinating Folio of Feasible Functions. The class came alive; no, it sang. The exercise Bob had chosen for the day was his adaptation for the class of a problem presented in Edward De Bono's *Five-Day Logic Course* (New York: NAL). Here's how it went . . .

— SELF OBSERVATION —

How do you solve problems?
  a. logical analysis?
  b. trial and error?
  c. insight?
  d. a combination of the above

Carefully observe and <u>analyze</u> your solutions to the Block Problems:
  1. Arrange the six blocks so that one is touching* exactly one other.
  2. So that one is touching* exactly two others.
  3. Three others
  4. Four others
  5. Five others

* For purposes of this problem, "touching" means that two <u>surfaces</u> are touching... not two edges... and not a surface and an edge.

← Touching ↑

Not Touching ↗

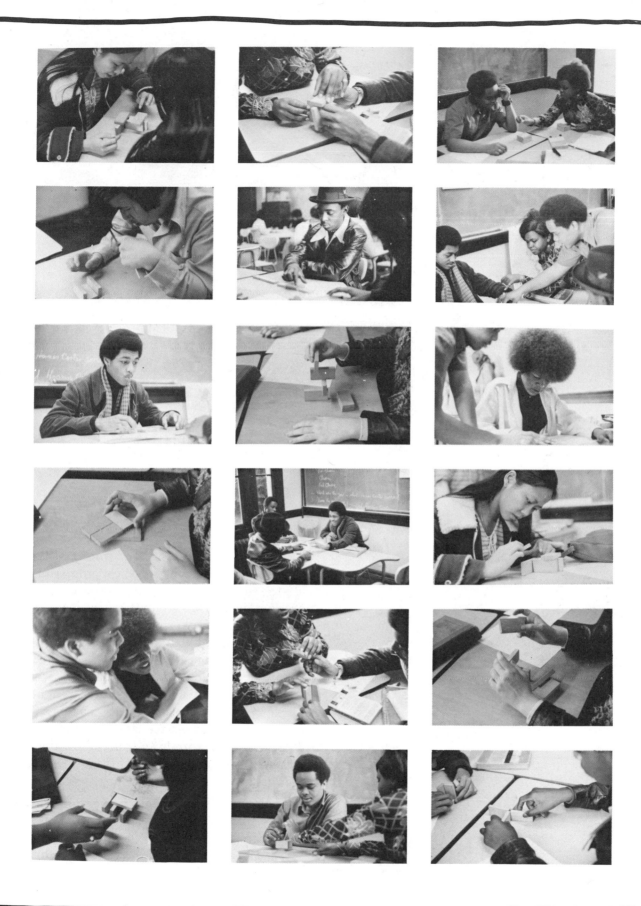

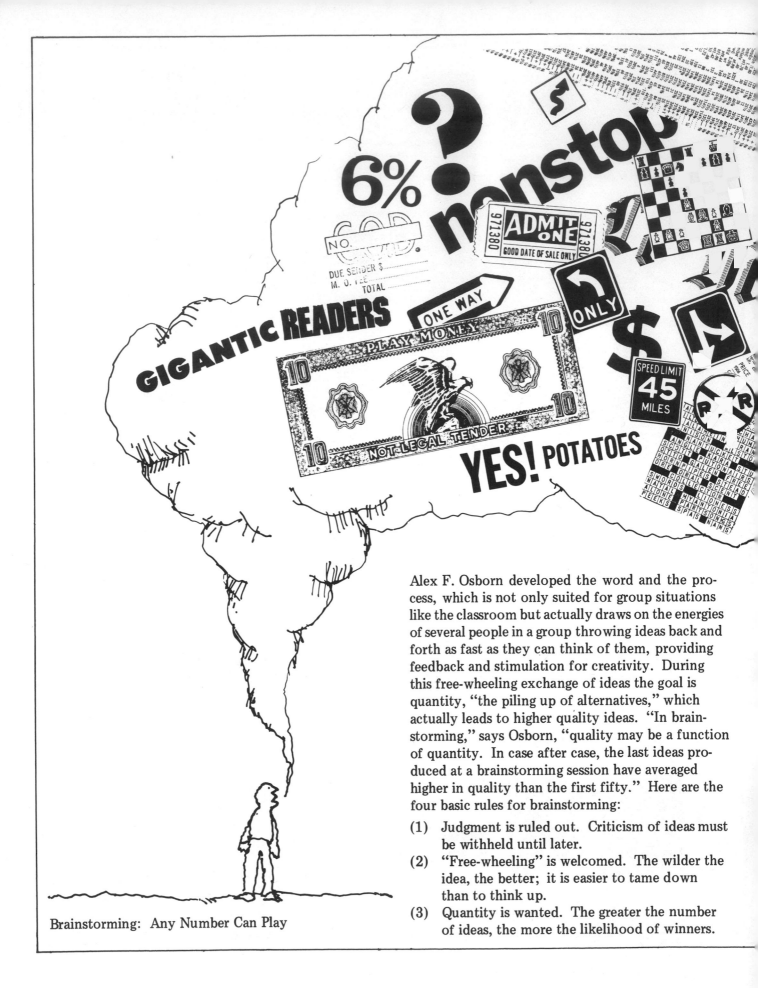

6% ? nonstop

GIGANTIC READERS

ONE WAY

ADMIT ONE
GOOD DATE OF SALE ONLY
971380

PLAY MONEY
10 10
10 10
NOT LEGAL TENDER

ONLY

$

SPEED LIMIT
45
MILES

YES! POTATOES

Brainstorming: Any Number Can Play

Alex F. Osborn developed the word and the process, which is not only suited for group situations like the classroom but actually draws on the energies of several people in a group throwing ideas back and forth as fast as they can think of them, providing feedback and stimulation for creativity. During this free-wheeling exchange of ideas the goal is quantity, "the piling up of alternatives," which actually leads to higher quality ideas. "In brainstorming," says Osborn, "quality may be a function of quantity. In case after case, the last ideas produced at a brainstorming session have averaged higher in quality than the first fifty." Here are the four basic rules for brainstorming:

(1) Judgment is ruled out. Criticism of ideas must be withheld until later.
(2) "Free-wheeling" is welcomed. The wilder the idea, the better; it is easier to tame down than to think up.
(3) Quantity is wanted. The greater the number of ideas, the more the likelihood of winners.

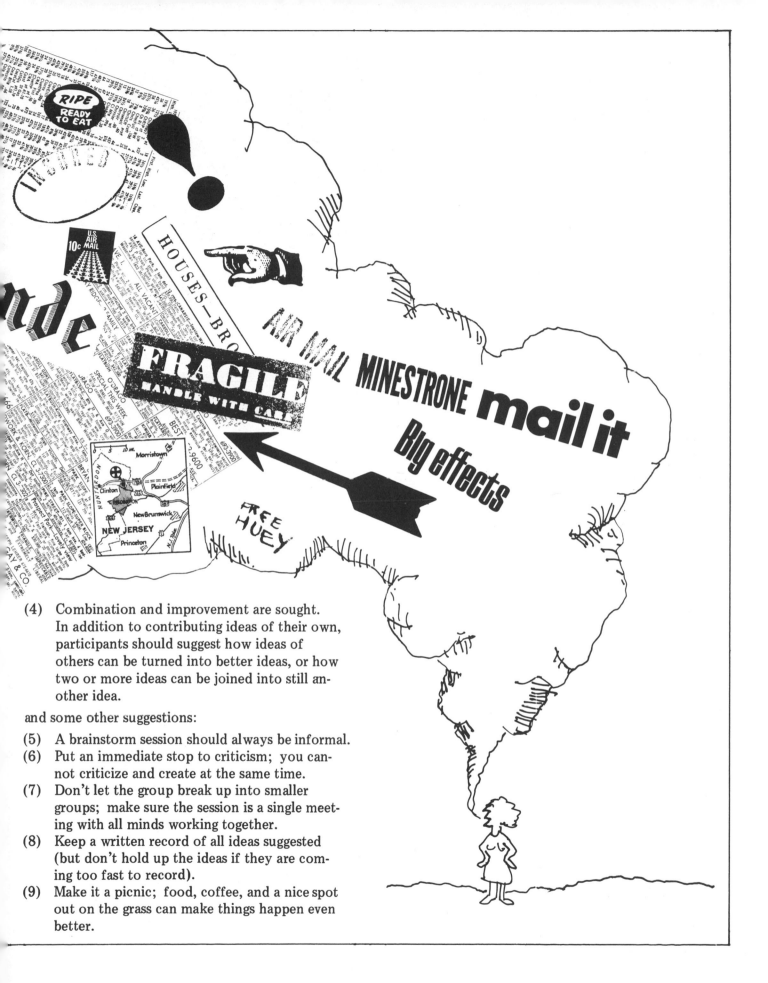

(4) Combination and improvement are sought.
In addition to contributing ideas of their own,
participants should suggest how ideas of
others can be turned into better ideas, or how
two or more ideas can be joined into still another idea.

and some other suggestions:

(5) A brainstorm session should always be informal.
(6) Put an immediate stop to criticism; you cannot criticize and create at the same time.
(7) Don't let the group break up into smaller
groups; make sure the session is a single meeting with all minds working together.
(8) Keep a written record of all ideas suggested
(but don't hold up the ideas if they are coming too fast to record).
(9) Make it a picnic; food, coffee, and a nice spot
out on the grass can make things happen even
better.

WEITZMAN'S FUNKY FOSSILS

or, Concrete Concepts from Cardboard Cutouts

The manipulation of physical data is a very real activity, not just for the physical scientist but for social scientists as well, particularly for those at the intersection of both, such as the anthropologist, archaeologist, or art historian. This is one of the reasons for introducing activities like Five Squares or problem solving with blocks. Another reason is to provide experience with solving problems in groups, the brainstorming of original ideas and hypotheses. I had these two things in the back of my mind when I approached the problem of how to get ninth and tenth grade students to understand the relationship between structure and function in living things, particularly the way that new environ-

ments and functions have shaped human structure. One place this might lead to, for example, is the understanding of variations in human populations.

It seemed to me that one of the things that might work would be to simulate the collection, reconstruction, and analysis of fossil remains and to place students in the same kind of situation faced by physical anthropologists. But how to do this? Skull casts are expensive. Specimens are available to us in the museum, but they're not for touching and certainly not to be removed to the classroom. I guessed finally that I was going to have to create my own "remains," or what a student would later label "Weitzman's funky fossils."

I.

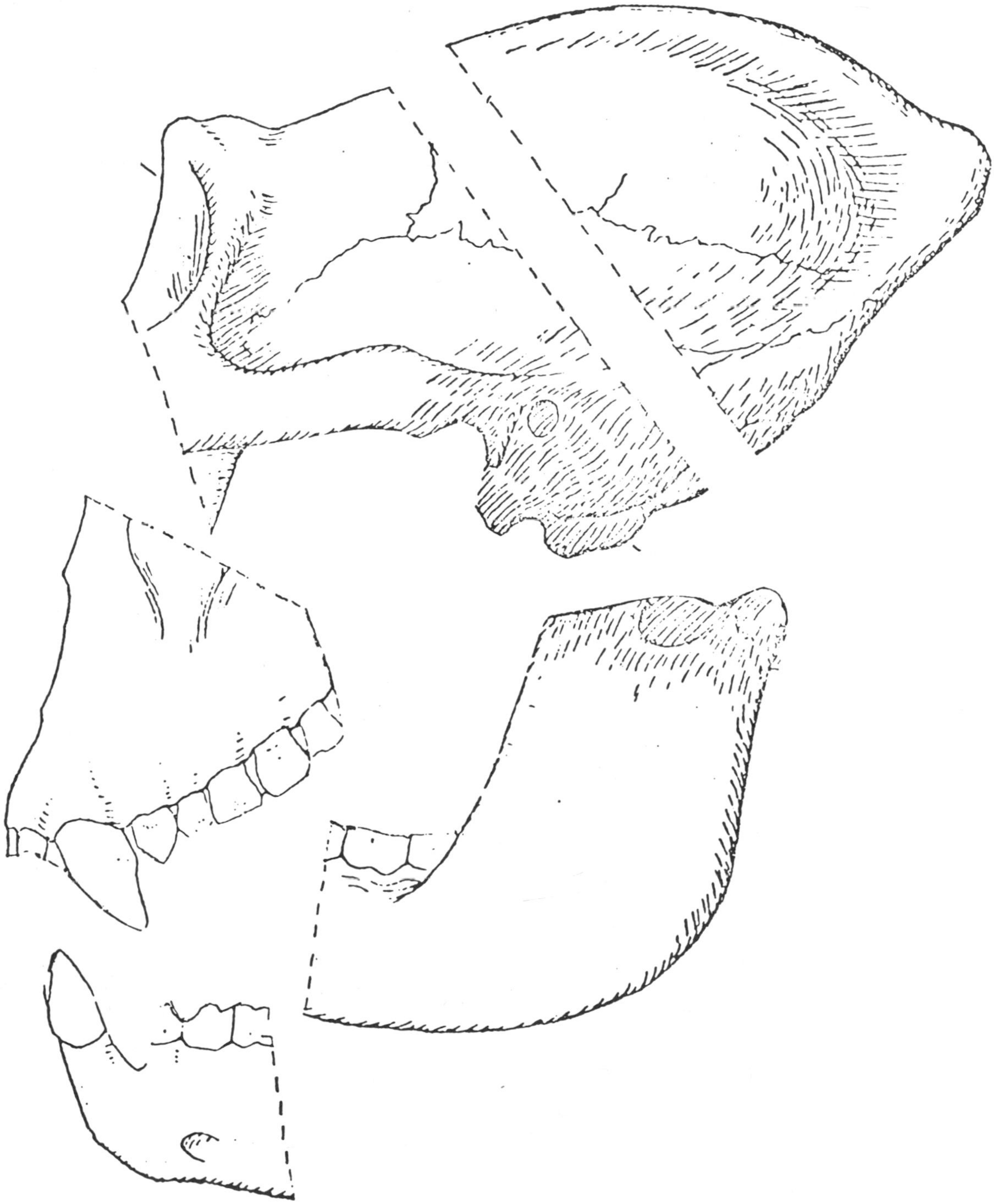

Here's how to put it together.

(1) I chose four skulls which, though somewhat generalized, can be identified as follows: The first is that of a modern ape; the second is *Australopithecus*, who lived about a million years ago; the third is *Sinanthropus pekinensis* (or Peking man), who lived about 500,000 years ago; and the fourth is modern man, *Homo sapiens*. *(Do not tell students what they are).*

(2) Using some copy process, make a set of four skulls for every three students in the class.

(3) Cut out the parts (simulating fragmentation), mix them up and place them in an envelope—one envelope of skull parts for each team of anthropologists. Parts will have a better "feel" and last longer if they are dry-mounted or rubber-cemented to heavy cardboard and then cut out with a razor blade. (I mounted mine on pressed wood and then cut them up on a jigsaw.)

(4) After organizing into teams (anyway you like), give each team a set of fragments and these instructions:

(a) Assemble the fragments you have "found."

(b) Arrange the completed reconstructions in what you think to be the order of their evolution or development, from the oldest to the most recent.

(c) Through comparison and discussion among you decide if all of your specimens are human. If you determine that they are all human, leave them in sequence as you have them. If you determine that one or more specimens are not human, separate them from the others.

(d) Finally, compile a field report describing your finds, observed similarities and differences in their structure, your "dating" of them and reasons for ordering in this way, and describing any changes you've noted from one to the next.

(e) Working by yourself now, complete the following parts of the study: If any of the specimens were rejected as not being human, explain why. If you did not agree with the decision of the others in the group, give your reasons.

Choose one of the patterns of change you observed and develop an hypothesis explaining why you think that change occurred.

(5) Allow time for each team to report their findings in class. (It's helpful to have overhead transparencies of the skulls to project and mark on as reports are presented.) Discuss the findings and the hypotheses for any observed changes.

2.

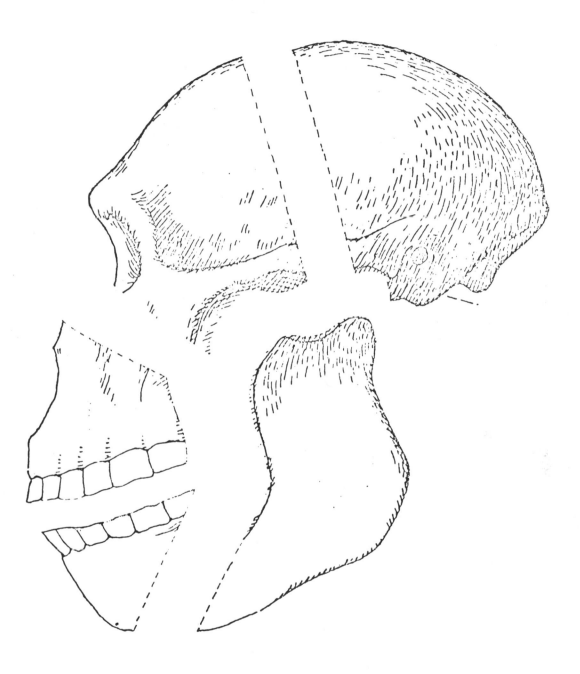

3.

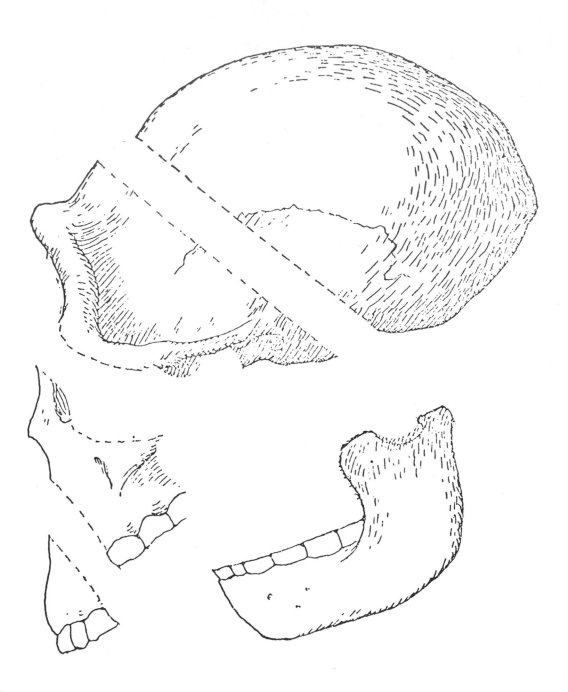

4.

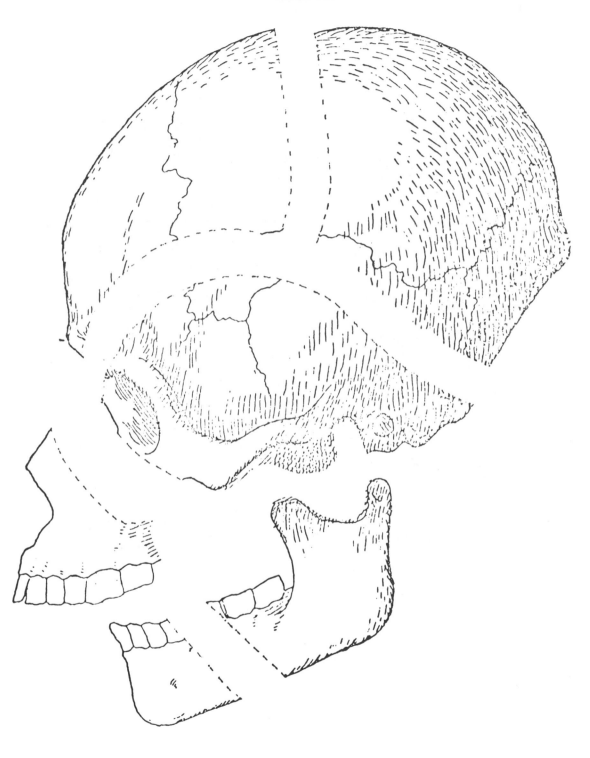

The Negative Image

We have grown accustomed to Images—printed, sketched, drawn, painted, carved, fashioned or electronic—and the way they fill our lives. For the moment try to imagine yourself among some distant, isolated people for whom you are to recreate American life using only spoken and written language. How far do you think you could get with words alone? What kinds of impressions of life in the United States could you convey without pictures of automobiles or Los Angeles or a television set, without movies or a signboard or ads from magazines, American paintings and sculpture, examples of architecture and design, without pictures of airplanes, diesel locomotives, trucks, earth moving machinery, a telephone, a computer, or even pictures of Americans themselves?

The image would become a bit clearer if you were to suggest that these people read some poetry, short stories, newspaper and magazine feature articles and reportage, and novels describing life in America. Still the final result would be impressions quite shallow if not meaningless, thoroughly informed but lacking in essence and color. But we needn't speculate on the outcome of such a task, for the question is not a hypothetical one. Such attempts are going on in lots of classrooms every day. Lots of words and precious little essence.

Color American education bland, monochromatic and dull; the grey of the printed page.

For lots of reasons Americans have a thing about written and spoken language, and the results of this are everywhere. Precise use of English is valued above poetic, colorful, individualized expression—and so, it's emphasized in school. Technical competency is valued above creativity—and so it's emphasized in school. Convergent thinking over divergent thinking, conformity over individuality; over and over and over we see the marks of a society which emphasizes above all the skill, mastery, and manipulation—within strict technical limits—of a written language.

Anthropologists have long been aware of the differences between societies that are literate and societies that are illiterate or pre-literate. For instance, while we may not think of it that way any longer, writing is a technical skill, which we begin to develop when we encourage children to pick up a crayon or a pencil to draw and scribble. It continues on in school when, beginning at about the age of seven, children learn to write. They learn to develop precise, muscular control in their hands in order to write, and then throughout their entire school career they are expected to use pencils and pens and, to a lesser extent, to draw. In a primitive society, where there is no written language, the child at the same age, at a very early age, is given perhaps a knife with which to carve images so that by the time a European or an American child is writing or using a pencil or a pen with fair skill the child in a pre-literate society has learned to use a knife or some other kind of carving tool. The end result is that children in Europe or America eventually learn to express themselves reasonably well using the conventional symbols of the language. On the other hand, the child growing up in the primitive society learns to express himself equally well with the conventional symbols of art.

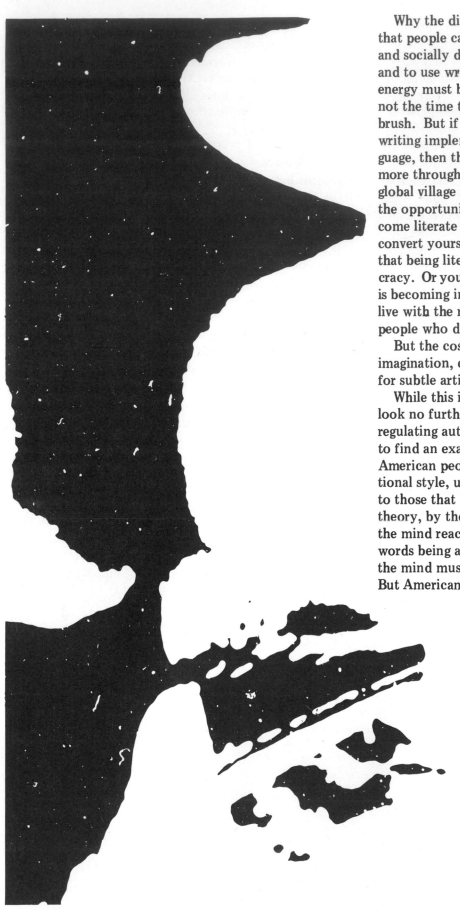

Why the difference? It's beginning to appear that people cannot do both. If it's economically and socially desirable for a child to learn to write and to use writing implements, then a great deal of energy must be spent in writing, and there just is not the time to learn to use a knife or a paint brush. But if there is no pressure to learn to use a writing implement because there is no written language, then the child expresses himself more and more through tools, through art. A fact of the global village is that more and more societies have the opportunity to make this choice. You can become literate and learn someone else's language, or convert yours into symbols and enjoy everything that being literate brings with it, including technocracy. Or you can retain your traditionalism, which is becoming increasingly more difficult to do, and live with the reputation of being a quaint, exotic people who do interesting carvings and paintings.

But the cost of literacy is very high—the loss of imagination, colorful expression, and the feeling for subtle artistic values.

While this is going to sound facetious, one need look no further than the current transition in signs regulating automobile traffic in the United States to find an example of the effect of literacy on the American people. The conversion is to an international style, using instead of words symbols similar to those that Europeans have used for years. The theory, by the way, is that in situations of danger the mind reacts faster to images than to words, words being an intermediate step through which the mind must go to get from reality to reaction. But Americans don't believe it; for them the process cannot be completed without going through a costly transitional stage during which signs will have to include both words and images. Traffic engineers, apparently, are afraid that we will confuse big red octagons with other features of the scenery, so to make sure we don't the big white letters, STOP, are added—the implication being, I suppose, that otherwise Americans would not stop. This is also true for large red and white inverted triangles which must abound in such numbers in the American landscape that some of them must bear the word YIELD to be recognized.

Language, and the American preoccupation with the word, is one of the most important determinants of American society and culture. In spite of the technology of imagery, which has come about largely through American innovation, the printed word— black type on white paper—is still the most often used, indeed the only trusted, communication medium for Americans. If you're not certain of this for the society generally, you cannot doubt that the printed word is the essential fact of education and that children live or die in the education system on the basis of how well they can read and write. While a picture might be worth a thousand words, it seems that teachers would rather take the chance with the thousand words, going on to maybe two or three thousand words if necessary. If this is true, then the evidence suggests that Americans are losing uniquely human and probably instinctive traits —their imaginations and their ability to express themselves in creative ways.

But let's assume for the moment that it has not happened and that we retain at least a vestigial imag-

109

ination. How then can we explain the fact that art and imagery count for so little with us, particularly in education? I think there are probably several complicated but easily identifiable reasons for this bias in American education, all of which, not surprisingly, reflect the attitudes of the larger society. First, it goes without saying that art is not central to American life. I don't believe there has ever been a period in American history when art and artists were central to the American experience, though one might argue, as does Tom Wolfe, that the automobile is the only unique American folk art form. But in its usual sense, art to most Americans is something that exists entirely for its beauty or for the aesthetic expression it conveys and is therefore consigned to the shelf with 'beautiful' things, being somehow superficial, aesthetic—which in America is sometimes synonymous with the effete—decorative, and most damning of all, effeminate. Art has strong social associations in America, as evidenced by the self-conscious artiness and quest for culture that marks the aspiring, upwardly mobile American. As a people we don't seem to feel the need to surround ourselves with beautiful things, and though we do like the things we use to be colorful, we demand only that they be functional and, more recently, that they don't injure us. Despite hopeful signs in the work of the Shakers and other of our early American ancestors, Americans have failed by and large to produce a synthesis of their very unique mode of life in some functional art form. American furniture and home furnishings can best be described as 1950 Sears or post-industrial drab for much of Middle America, and for those with money,

taste, and aspirations, Mussolini modern or period plastic.

Now, it is possible that our art consists of all the things we manufacture and consume, but if all these things are indeed our art and art is supposed to be some kind of expression, some kind of spiritual expression, then I can only conclude from this that we have some very strange gods. It is significant that the one art form in which Americans have been truly creative is architecture, an expression of the aesthetic which possesses both form and function, a synthesis which Americans, as noted before, not only understand and appreciate but worship as a virtue.

This brings us to another factor—the image of artists and their role in American society. The artist too lives at the periphery of our lives, to most Americans a childlike figure who still dabbles in paints and clays, the stuff of our childhood. We do not take artists very seriously, and in the Middle American mind at least, the stereotypical artist in his paint-smeared pants and messy studio appears irresponsible, rebellious, promiscuous, anarchic, and, worst of all, unkempt. Artists are bohemians to the American mind and as such are not really to be believed. Of course, like architects, there are some establishment artists, like Norman Rockwell for example, who have not only gained acceptance but have attained the status of minor saints.

In any case, people who produce art are certainly not as important in the American scheme as people who produce machines and weapons. If this strikes you as being sort of warmed-over radical rhetoric, consider the fact that while most Americans can identify

Andrew Carnegie, John D. Rockefeller, and Henry Ford with their accomplishments, few have even heard of Thomas Eakins, or Edward Hopper or Jackson Pollack, or Georgia O'Keefe, and the name Remington is more likely to be associated with arms manufacture than with paintings and sculpture evoking the life of the American western frontier.

I remember my very first day in graduate school at Northwestern, when Franklin D. Scott asked us to write down the names of ten people who we believed most influenced the course of human history. Of the seventy or eighty names we offered up, most were of political figures (Hitler, Churchill, Roosevelt, Lenin), a few were spiritual leaders (Mohammed, Christ, Luther, Marx), two were scientists (Copernicus and Einstein), and only one was an artist—Picasso. Professor Scott has made his point about our concept of history. The artist, as well as the artist within us, then, has not only been excluded from our lives, but has effectively been excluded from our history and our consciousness as well.

Also, there is the image projected by museums and museum people themselves that greatly affects our view of art. Of course, the only place we really see art is tucked away somewhere in a museum. I know a museum director, for instance, who regards his museum as a "temple of beauty," and while he is certainly right in a sense he has, I think, missed the greater sense of art. In the same way, one might describe a highly efficient manufacturing plant in the United States as a "monument to American ingenuity," which would also be correct, but also misses the point. Inside a factory there is a hell of a lot more going on. In his book *Museum Without*

Walls Andre Malraux notes that the museum is first of all a Western invention, not having existed anywhere in Asia, nor anywhere outside of Europe, for that matter, where European civilization had not touched. And secondly, that the museum is a fairly recent phenomenon, even in Western history. One of Malraux's conclusions is that the museum has been more influential than any other factor in Western life in determining what art is and is not to us. I think the implication of all this for us as teachers lies in the title of that book, *Museum Without Walls*, because we will have to rediscover the essential values of art beyond its jewel-like presentation in the museum. We must remember that for many of the peoples of the world and for virtually all of the world's primitive or pre-literate people art holds an entirely different meaning than it does for us. We tend to project the role of art and the artist in American society onto other cultures, past and present, assuming in our ethnocentric way that it must be the same for them too. Yet the fact is that in most primitive societies art is not only central to the lives of the people, it is so central that it is not even looked upon as art, not even identifiable as something separate from their lives. Instead, it is real life, an expression of religious faith or of cultural continuity. The question for us is, then, can we convey this to students, can we re-kindle in the child's mind the true meaning of what we call a work of art? I think we can, and I think the way we can do this is to begin by using the museum in a way that will call attention to the real meaning of art and the way it was originally used. To do this we need to ask the right questions.

The Museum Trip

After schools, museums are the most misunderstood and misused places in the world. It's little wonder that a great many Americans regard them much as they do subway stations and railroad terminals, the one place where there is certain to be a public toilet, even on Sundays.

Consider a child's first experience with a museum. It is likely to begin amidst a herd of forty or fifty kids fused into a mass somewhere in the bowels of a giant yellow bus. Squished through the doors, the flowing human stream pours into the museum behind an adult who, at first glance, seems to be leading this whole affair but is in actuality being driven ahead by the fear of faltering and falling under their feet. Somewhere in the museum, now, the child-mass (dragging coats, sweaters, purses, gym shoes, and tin lunch buckets along the stone floors) is perfunctorily introduced to a guide whose name had just a few minutes before been drawn from a hat to see who would take the group—and she had lost! But her defeat was only a temporary setback, for now, taking advantage of the momentum the child-mass has gained, presumably from being forceably expelled from the bus, she raises her arm overhead in a signal and hurls the throng into the gallery, where it approaches, momentarily engulfs, and pours around, over, and between statues, glass cases, pedestals, benches, and frail humans, like some awesome, groaning, humming amoeba,

trailing in its wake scattered clues of its passing—mittens, shreads of Kleenex, a spilled bag of M&M's, two bus transfers, and a badly chewed pencil.

Standing at rest now, the group looks for all the world like people crammed into one of those elevators with two doors, looking anxiously in every direction, not sure where it's going to happen. Being in the center of the group affords an excellent view of the ceiling and the heads of taller pieces of sculpture. Some of the class can actually hear what the guide is reciting and a very few can actually see the tiny blue scarab taken from the tomb of Tutankhamen. "Are there any questions?" But before most of the kids have even seen the thing the guide is gliding silently across the floor, leading on, tantalizing her great restless monster whose hundreds of eyes are fixed straight ahead, which twists and turns its way through Gallery A and Gallery C (in Gallery B there are Tantric dieties, gods and goddesses locked togeth . . . well, let's just skip Gallery B), until it seems they are on a collision course with the great stone Bodhisattva from Angkor Wat. Walkie-talkie wearing guards have joined them now, cryptic, garbled radio messages emanating from somewhere under their suit jackets as they circle the group to make sure that no one breaks loose and strays from the herd, or worse—TOUCHES SOMETHING.

with them once you get them there? Those are putting-you-on-the-spot kinds of questions which provoke self-conscious replies like "I want to expand my students' horizons," or "It is essential that they be able to recognize in medieval and Renaissance art salient variations in style and execution," bullshit kinds of answers which cover up for real answers like "I don't know . . . I just want to get them out and away, and museums are one of the places we can get out and away." I like to take kids to museums just to let them *be* there, for us to be there together. It's nice going somewhere without an adult planning every minute of your day, and I can remember as a kid trying to "lose" my mom and dad or my teacher so that I could pretend, at least, to be there by myself, to be myself in a big new place. New places require getting used to, and too often we take kids to a museum or some other place they've never been before for an hour or two and expect them to confine their attention to a couple of rooms or the limited path of a tour guide, when their minds and curiosities are actually running all over the place. Let them explore and be on their own. How would you feel being taken to a wondrous new place, guided quickly through only the part somebody else wants you to see, and then being whisked out the door and back home?

After they've had a chance to explore, after they're comfortable in a new place—*then* you think about things to learn and talk about. One of my reasons for taking kids to museums is to help them use what's there to make contact with other people, people just like themselves only far away. I'm not concerned with "teaching" aesthetics and all that, and I'm not interested in making art critics out of them. I want to give them a way to use any museum anywhere and what's in it—painting, sculpture, carvings, photographs, masks, clothing, implements—to glean from them anything they want to know or feel, to do things with art in a comfortable, intuitive way.

This use of museums and galleries to explore the ways of peoples and to learn something of their lives and beliefs and fears and hopes and humor and sexuality and every other kind of thing, I call . . . art as artifact.

Art as artifact is looking at, touching and feeling a thing, going back through its contours and textures and colors to the hands and tools of the woman or man who made it, back through the body and mind, and back to the eyes, to look through

Fortunately, I was spared this kind of abuse as a child, but I have seen it enough times to be able to understand why many children don't want to return to the museum. I know a lot of sensitive teachers who are appalled by this kind of scene and have given up, yet feel as I do that museums are beautiful places, points of contact with the past and with present things from elsewhere, a place where you can get in touch with all the feelings people have ever had. The museum has many answers to our personal thoughts about what we are, where we have been, and where we are likely to be going. Children should be introduced to these delights, and there is another way . . . .

But first, why do you want to take kids to a museum anyway, and what are you going to do

them and see the world ten thousand miles from here or a million years ago, back to times and places I've never been, could never be, seen and expressed by another person who was there. I think of a wooden carving or a stone sculpture or a painting as the "now" of a hundred years ago, a moment in time kept alive, an offering from someone who had something to say, who wanted to reach out and touch me.

It is probably for these reasons that I like to introduce kids to primitive and ancient things; they're more direct, more personal, in a way. Oh, I like modern things too—Voulkos pipes, Moore's mammoth matrons, and Magritte's locomotives steaming out of the fireplace; they're fun. But they are also so intellectual, so slick and refined . . . so impersonal . . . so dead when compared to primitives. It's like the difference between Thomas Mann and Richard Brautigan. The expressions of simpler people seem to provide clearer—though not always less complicated—insights into human nature. And we can do so much more with them. We can project backwards, back thousands of years, to sharpen our images and enliven our fantasies of what it was like to be alive then. Or if we're into a behavioral thing we can learn so much about elemental emotions, attitudes, customs, social conventions, what people thought about when they fell in love or what fathers and mothers and children did together and talked about, or what happened when you got sick or died, and where your spirit is and where it goes. Anyway, I'm tired of the usual focus of "history" and of the elite literates of highly-developed civilizations. I can't relate to these people. I like the people who, because they moved around a lot to find food, or lived in the bush or some isolated valley, were too busy living to devote much time to building pyramids and steam engines and trying out all kinds of ways of annihilating their neighbors.

Ten years ago, when I began teaching, art to me was European art and American art, or those few graphic and plastic forms European and American critics regard as art. But somehow I went through a conversion, or what we might now call the greening of a teacher, which I think is worth sharing, particularly if you are now where I was then. If you've travelled (as I hadn't, then), or if you've taken courses in anthropology (as I hadn't), or if you've read a lot about Eskimos, or Native Americans, or Balinese, or Bushmen (as I hadn't), you'll probably find this a little tedious. But here goes

. . . the first step, or, how to know something about something you don't know anything about.

As I said, I knew nothing about primitive or ancient art. But I was intrigued by primitive people and found, as many of you did, that more and more my world history class was evolving into a world cultures class, and that more and more the world cultures class was becoming more democratic, more concerned with people, the kinds of people Berthold Brecht wrote about. Part of it was some of the new things which suddenly appeared in the '60's, like the *Anthropology Curriculum Study Project*, the *Asian Studies Inquiry Program*, and *Man: A Course of Study*. Part of it was that some anthropologists and historians were becoming more interested in kids and schools. All of a sudden teachers were meeting new people. I listened to Bob Hanvey, Fred Gearing, and Kurt Johnson talk about kids and fossils and peasants. I once found myself standing between Sherwood Washburn and Robert Adams making small talk about Land Rovers, Jeeps, and digging in the sands of Iraq for ancient cities, and at another time being with those two beautiful mavericks in the very academic world of anthropology, John Collier and John Connally . . . .

But we were talking about art. I realized I didn't have any words for expressing to my students what I wanted to say, a vocabulary that would allow me to articulate ideas, to describe a particular piece, or, more important, to ask questions. I felt then as many of us do now when we try to say something intelligent about a film: somehow the usual adjectives don't work, and it comes to "I liked it . . . " or "It had a certain quality about it . . ." or "It all held together." A whole new vocabulary is needed. So I began to look for some information, interpretations, and—although I didn't know it at the time —some strategies for approaching art in a useful way and helping kids do the same.

Now, I seemed to have two choices of sources. One was large picture books with lots of slick pictures, lots of dull copy, and few insights. The other was something by an anthropologist or an art historian, which usually has lots of insights but few slick pictures. Pictures abound in this world of ours, but insights are rare indeed, so I opted for an anthropologist and very happily found among some of the dullest, most pedantic writing in the world an article which said a lot in a small space and left lots of room for thought. As I began taking notes, a strategy emerged which, perhaps, you'll see . . .

114

"ART IN A CULTURAL CONTEXT" E. R. LEACH (IN PETER HAMMOND'S CULTURAL AND SOCIAL ANTHROPOLOGY, MACMILLAN, pp. 344-350)

PRIMITIVE ART COMES IN AN IMMENSE VARIETY OF FORMS AND MATERIALS

> BUSHMAN ROCK PAINTINGS
> ESKIMO BONE CARVINGS
> FIJIAN BARK-CLOTH PRINTS
> DECORATED ANCESTRAL SKULLS — NEW GUINEA
> AZTEC, MAYAN STONE CARVINGS
> PREHISTORIC PERUVIAN POTTERY
> WEST AFRICAN CAST METAL WORK

THE FORM AND CONTENT OF ANY PLASTIC ART IS CONDITIONED BY THE MEDIUM THROUGH WHICH IT IS EXPRESSED.

IN PRIMITIVE SOCIETY THE MEDIUM OF ARTISTIC EXPRESSION IS PARTLY DETERMINED BY ENVIRONMENT

THE DISTINCTION BETWEEN "CRAFTMANSHIP" AND THE ARTIST AS SPECIALIST, AS A PROFESSIONAL, DOES NOT APPLY.

* THE GREAT BULK OF PRIMITIVE ART IS DEFINITELY REPRESENTATIONAL RATHER THAN ABSTRACT IT IS INTENDED TO BE UNDERSTOOD

* PRIMITIVE ART IS NOT A UNITY — EACH LOCAL CULTURAL GROUP HAS ITS OWN AESTHETIC TRADITIONS PECULIAR TO THAT GROUP, CONVENTIONS

PRINCIPAL MARKETS FOR PRODUCTS OF PRIMITIVE ARTISTS —
RELIGIOUS, CEREMONIAL FURNISHINGS
DECORATION OF HOUSES, BOATS, AND PERSONAL BELONGINGS OF IMPORTANT PERSONS
MEMORIALS FOR THE CELEBRATED DEAD
(CF. WESTERN ARTIST - CHURCH AND PRIVATE PATRON)

* THE AUDIENCE FOR WHICH A PRIMITIVE ARTIST WORKS IS COMPOSED OF MEMBERS OF HIS OWN COMMUNITY, STEEPED IN THE SAME MYTHOLOGICAL TRADITIONS, FAMILIAR WITH THE SAME ENVIRONMENT OF MATERIAL FACT AND RITUAL ACTIVITY — CONVENTIONS AND SYMBOLS.

ACTIVITY: CONVENTIONS/MATERIALS/"PUBLIC" ART

* WE HAVE COME TO THINK OF BOTH THE PRACTICE AND ENJOYMENT OF THE ARTS AS PRIVATE PURSUITS.

IN PRIMITIVE SOCIETY PRIVACY IS SELDOM VALUED; THE ARTS ARE AN ADORNMENT FOR PUBLIC FESTIVITY

115

My next problem was how to translate this into an activity that would make it all real. And it was at this point that I became aware of some assumptions that I had been making all along that simply were not true. One assumption on my part was that kids just naturally "see." I mean, they have eyes, after all, and if you just give them the opportunity to look at something they'll see in it what there is to see. But children must be taught to see, and acquiring this insight (it only took about five years) was also part of my greening. Being aware of this was the first stage. The next was to devise a way of helping children to see or, more specifically, to order and organize their percepts from the incredible array of input and stimuli we receive through our eyes and then to use these percepts, now ordered and arranged, to perform any of the several tasks we might ask of them, such as describing, comparing, or probing for values and mores, or even enjoying. We cannot, for example, just tell children to go to the museum, look at two pieces of sculpture or several paintings, and "compare" them. "Comparing" is a complex process requiring at least

(1) seeing all there is to see in the piece (color, form, contour, style, shapes, textures),

(2) recognizing differences and similarities in one or several of these attributes, and

(3) verbalizing, describing the observed qualities, differences, and similarities.

Because not all students are capable of performing these steps, and because the degree of competence in any of them varies from student to student and class to class, the teacher is constantly involved in diagnosis and training. Some students can accomplish the first step with ease, but not the other two. Others can perform the first two steps, but a limited vocabulary or ability to articulate ideas makes it seem at first that they are unable to do any of the steps. Some students who appear unable to complete even the first step are actually seeing and comparing but are unable to articulate their percepts because of a limited vocabulary. The point is that in this or any other task we give to students the teacher must be sensitive to student needs, providing direction when necessary as to what to look for or helping to find the words and phrases which help the students express what they've seen and what they are feeling.

For example, I remember an exchange one day at the Asian Art Museum in San Francisco. We were looking at some very early Chinese pottery vessels which illustrated the progression over many centuries from crude unfired pots to glazed ones. While we were standing in front of the case, I asked a student a question about the pots that required comparison and generation of some new ideas. But I discovered that I had jumped too far ahead and would have to go back . . .

Eddie, what do these pots tell us about what's happening to these people, what changes are occurring in their culture?

The symbol-making function is one of man's primary activities, like eating, looking, or moving about. It is the fundamental process of his mind, and goes on all the time. Sometimes we are aware of it, sometimes we merely find its results, and realize that certain experiences have passed through our brains and have been digested there . . .
Susane K. Langer

116

[No response . . . Eddie obviously understands my question, but it requires a series of intermediate steps he cannot organize or perform, and I've asked him to do too much at one time.]

OK, let's all look at that pot on the left there. Eddie, can you describe the pot, tell me something about its color and shape and . . .

Well, it's gray all over. It doesn't look like it's made very well, I mean it's rough and, you know, not very good . . . crude, it's out of shape . . . and it's not very pretty.

All right, how about the other pot; how would you describe that?

It's smooth . . . it's got some kind of painted design on it . . . zigzags or something . . . painted, I think, the paint's chipped off . . . it looks really old . . .

Great, which do you think is older?

I think the first one . . . the first pot looks lots older.

Are the pots *similar* in any way; are they the *same* in any way?

Uh . . . both are round . . . pot shaped . . . like those Indian pots you showed us last week. [Eddie has just made a comparison acknowledged by anthropologists as evidence of the Asian origins of Native Americans.]

OK, so you've now compared the two pots and you find . . .

This second pot here seems to be better made, it's smooth and shiny . . . glazed, and it has a design painted on it. Both are round, like pots always are.

Does this tell you anything about the people who made them?

. . . . I suppose it means that they're getting better at it, they're learning to do new things with clay and paint . . . they're trying out new things . . . new colors and things . . .

And so are you, Eddie. Look at what Eddie's done. First, he has demonstrated his ability to make accurate, careful observations. With a little help he is able to classify and order them and then make some simple comparisons. And finally, he is able to formulate a hypothesis on why these two pots are different. In the process, this kid has hit upon one of the great archeological discoveries (similarities in Old World and New World culture) and, as if this were not enough in a few minutes, has discovered a universal, "pot-ness," the fact that all pots everywhere look pretty much like pots.

Does the fact that the Chinese and Indian pots look alike surprise you at all? Doesn't that seem strange?

No . . . No, that's not strange. Look, a pot's a pot, no matter where it is, it's a pot . . . it does things pot's are supposed to do . . . I mean . . . like a car, right? It doesn't matter where a car is made, it's got to look like a car and all, it's got to have wheels, and it's got to have doors, and it's got to have seats inside . . .

The symbol is essentially the expression of the child's present reality.

Jean Piaget

I'll have Eddie on my archeological team anytime.

While some would criticize my emphasis on speculation, I think it's important that kids have the chance to guess too. Why should adults have all the fun just because they call what they do something fancy like "hypothesis formulation?" Several museums were available to us, within easy reach. If I hadn't had them I could have done almost as well collecting pictures from books and magazines or making color slides of them.

Two ideas began shaping my plans at this point. First, I don't want to herd kids through a museum, lecturing, telling jokes, asking rhetorical questions, and playing Kenneth Clark. And I don't want anybody else doing it to them either. Secondly, I am more concerned with depth of understanding than just exposure. I want to concentrate at first on a few simple concepts which can be accomplished in about an hour, and still leave another hour for us to explore other parts of the museum, sit and talk over coffee in the cafeteria, and have a work session on the lawn while everything's fresh in our minds, all the impressions and ideas and questions. So, for the first visit to the museum I chose to get across these concepts . . .

(1) Primitive art all but defies definition (and, thus, stereotyping) in its variety of forms, subject, and media.

(2) There is a relationship between the medium of artistic expression and the environment from which it springs.

(3) Primitive artists, indeed artists in every society, tend to use certain conventions whose meaning were accepted and understood by all members of the society.

(4) Primitive objects were not intended for display or sale, but to be useful, to be used as furnishings, for religious and ceremonial purposes, as houses, boats, personal belongings, and

(5) Art is an artifact of life in ancient and distant places, a source of contact with others elsewhere in time and space.

To accomplish this in the time I intended meant carefully choosing pieces that would help students acquire these understandings on their own. Nothing is gained by exposing students to dozens of pieces; the goal should be a few pieces which illustrate the concepts you want to develop. So, visiting the museum I looked over the collections seeking pieces that would do it, and, then, after a few times through, I chose what I wanted, wrote down their descriptions, and made a rough map of the rooms showing the position of each piece and the corresponding number.

Finally, I added questions for the students to think about while they were looking at the pieces, and, like my questions to Eddie, which encouraged comparison with other pieces they had seen or would see. I had, in the end, a do-it-yourself guide to primitive art which students could follow themselves, alone or in small groups, as they chose, a field guide upon which they could sketch details,

The concept [word] is general and communicable, the image is singular and egocentric.

Jean Piaget

write their impressions, notes, and questions they wanted to raise later. Moving about the museum in this way, they were dispersed, less noticeable and quieter than a large group. They were able to spend as much time as they wanted to with each piece, were free to move back and forth between two or more pieces, could move along at their own rate, could come and get me if they wanted to talk about something, and were free to confer among themselves, compare notes, have a smoke, people-watch (which, I suggest to my classes, is one of the fun things to do in a museum) and enjoy the day.

The final step was a meeting, sitting in a circle on the grass, getting in touch with our impressions, what we saw and how we felt, what we liked, before all these beautiful things evaporated on the ride back to school. We made three other trips using similar guides, and additional guides were made for students who wanted to go to the museum on their own—and did—on Saturdays, Sundays, and cutting days.

Sitting on the grass with our shoes off in the sun, still feeling the things we had just seen and experienced, we just talked . . . .
Did you find the room that had the ancient fountain and the plants ? . . . Yeah, it was like being in a garden . . . and paintings all around . . . and nice sounds too, that gurgling water was the only nice sound in the museum . . . museums should have music . . . yeah, quiet rooms and music rooms . . . I like the quiet . . . I like sitting on that soft bench in the middle of the room just looking at the things

around, the paintings and old furniture and all, and the people . . .
What kinds of things did you see?
Masks . . . puppets . . . paintings . . . wood carvings . . . things made of metal . . . I saw old drums . . . and pots, pots everywhere . . . and dolls and little wooden figures; are those children's toys?
Let me tell you a little story about one of those dolls, the Ashanti doll . . . remember? . . . There it is, Patricia has made a really nice sketch of it, pass it around so we can look at it . . . Well, these dolls are worn and carried by Ashanti women when they're pregnant . . .
It's their baby, it's like their baby . . .
Right, Jennifer, it represents their unborn baby in a way, or the ideal baby. Remember when we talked about how people express the ideal in their art?
What's nice about being an artist is that no matter how screwed up the world is, you can create your own little ideal world . . .

More than anything else in experience, the arts mold our actual life of feeling . . . Few people realize that the real education of emotion is not the 'conditioning' effected by social approval and disapproval, but the tacit, personal, illuminating contact with symbols of feeling.

Susanne K. Langer

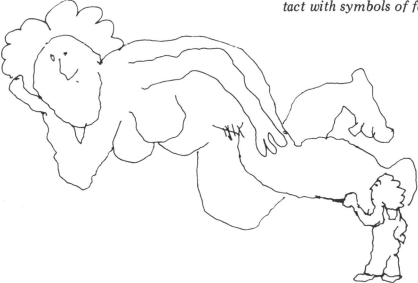

119

120

Like the Chinese artists, making all those perfect pictures of mountains and little houses . . . like gardens, more like gardens, planned out.

Yes, they were creating their own order, and this little doll represents the Ashanti ideal of a little girl or a woman. We have an image of the ideal child or person in our mind, don't we? I hear you talking about how people look; you're measuring them up against an ideal or standard you have of how a young man or young woman should look, right?

My mamma's pregnant, and she talks about the baby, and all. She wants a girl. She said she's tired of havin' boys around all the time . . .

My sister's goin' to have a baby and she's always sayin' that she want her to have fine hair like her father . . . and big eyes . . .

She's assuming it will be a little girl, then . . .

Yeah, you know, she likes little girls and she wants this first one to be a little girl . . . she says little boys are always gettin' into things, makin' trouble.

Well, I suspect the Ashanti women preferred little girls too, and this doll represents the kind of little girl they'd like to have. But, how do we know that this is an "ideal," how do we know it's not just one artist's idea . . . Willie?

They're all the same . . . like, there's lot's of them in that case and they're all alike, in a way . . .

What's that mean?

It's the sameness, it's what's the same about them that the women like . . . I don't know how to say it . . .

You're doing just fine. It *is* the "sameness."

When we see a lot of things that look alike that must mean that's their ideal or that convention thing . . .

OK, Tracy we're there; does everyone understand what Willie and Tracy have put together for us?

If we see a lot of paintings and carvings and things and parts of them all look alike even though they've been done by different people, then those parts that look alike are probably conventions . . .

Exactly. OK, now, assuming this is true in this case, what is the ideal child, female child, in the eyes of an Ashanti woman . . .

Thin and light . . . the doll's really smaller, more graceful than the other things . . . a long neck . . . a round head, well, more like the shape of an egg . . . narrow eyes . . . the head tapers toward the chin . . . a little face and narrow nose . . .

That's what *they* like, huh, Mr. Weitzman?
That's what *they* like Ronny.

121

. . . and making your own (museum)

I walked by Faye Das' open doors as I do every
morning on the way to my room across the hall,
only this time I stopped, mid-stride, to return the
stares of dozens of eyes, penetrating eyes, some
mirthful, some menacing, the haunting eyes of
masks. I felt at that moment the mystery and wonder that masks evoke, the strange powers of those
visages that have entranced people everywhere for
thousands of generations. Their contours and mood
were familiar, recalling images of Africa and Asia,
but the colors were fresh and spontaneous, so ex-
pressive of the magic breathed into them by their
young creators. Entering the room, a room I had
come to regard as the school's museum, I found
students deep into the making of magic . . .

with paper plates
and strips of newspaper
and flour paste
and tempera paints
and brushes
and picture books

and enjoying the "power of being the cause."

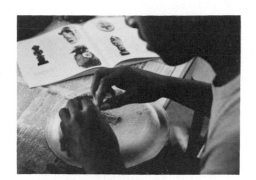

THE INVISIBLE PRESENT

The following excerpt is from the "Playboy Interview With Marshall McLuhan."

All media, from the phonetic alphabet to the computer, are extensions of man that cause deep and lasting changes in him and transform his environment. Such an extension is an intensification, an amplification of an organ, sense or function, and whenever it takes place, the central nervous system appears to institute a self-protective *numbing* of the affected area, insulating and anesthetizing it from conscious awareness of what's happening to it. It's a process rather like that which occurs to the body under shock or stress conditions, or to the mind in line with the Freudian concept of repression. I call this peculiar form of self-hypnosis Narcisus narcosis, a syndrome whereby man remains as unaware of the psychic and social effects of his new technology as a fish of the water it swims in. As a result, precisely at the point where a new media-induced environment becomes all pervasive and transmogrifies our sensory balance, it also becomes invisible.

This problem is doubly acute today because man must, as a simple survival strategy, become aware of what is happening to him, despite the attendant pain of such comprehension. The fact that he has not done so in this age of electronics is what has made this also the age of anxiety, which in turn has been transformed into its *Doppelganger*—the therapeutically reactive age of *anomie* and apathy. But despite our self-protective escape mechanisms, the total-field awareness engendered by electronic media is enabling us—indeed, compelling us—to grope toward a consciousness of the unconscious, toward a realization that technology is an extension of our own bodies. We live in the first age when change occurs sufficiently rapidly to make such pattern recognition possible for society at large. Until the present era, this awareness has always been reflected first by the artist, who has had the power—and courage—of the seer to read the language of the outer world and relate it to the inner world.

Inherent in the artist's creative inspiration is the process of subliminally sniffing out environmental change. It's always been the artist who perceives the alterations in man caused by a new medium, who recognizes that the future is the present, and uses his work to prepare the ground for it. But most people, from truck drivers to the literary Brahmins, are still blissfully ignorant of what the media do to them; unaware that because of their pervasive effects on man, it is the medium itself that is the message, *not* the content, and unaware that the medium is also the *massage*—that, all puns aside, it literally works over and saturates and molds and transforms every sense ratio. The content or message of any particular medium has about as much importance as the stenciling on the casing of an atomic bomb. But the ability to perceive media-induced extensions of man, once the province of the artist, is now being expanded as the new environment of electric information makes possible a new degree of perception and critical awareness by nonartists.

People are beginning to understand the nature of their new technology, but not yet nearly enough of them—and not nearly well enough. Most people, as I indicated, still cling to what I call the rearview-mirror view of their world. By this I mean to say that because of the invisibility of any environment during the period of its innovation, man is only consciously aware of the environment that has *preceded* it; in other words, an environment becomes fully visible only when it has been superseded by a new environment; thus we are always one step behind in our view of the world. Because we are benumbed by any new technology—which in turn creates a totally new environment—we tend to make the old environment more visible; we do so by turning it into an art form and by attaching ourselves to the objects and atmosphere that characterized it, just as we've done with jazz, and as we're now doing with the garbage of the mechanical environment via pop art.

The present is always invisible because it's environmental and saturates the whole field of attention so overwhelmingly; thus everyone but the artist, the man of integral awareness, is alive in an earlier day. In the midst of the electronic age of software, of instant information movement, we still believe we're living in the mechanical age of hardware. At the height of the mechanical age, man turned back to earlier centuries in search of "pastoral" values. The Renaissance and the Middle Ages were completely oriented toward Rome; Rome was oriented toward Greece, and the Greeks were oriented toward the pre-Homeric primitives. We reverse the old educational dictum of learning by proceeding from the familiar to the unfamiliar, by going from the unfamiliar to the familiar, which is nothing more or less than the numbing mechanism that takes place whenever new media drastically extend our senses.

Reality ReplayReplayRepl

It was just about two years ago that Bill Ames came to me as a student teacher and began working with a twelfth-grade class we called "The Thinking Circle," because we were going to be just that. Within a few weeks, however, our roles reversed and I became Bill's student teacher. One of the things he introduced me to that semester was the use of videotape. Not that I hadn't seen or used it before. I had used videotape for years as a self-evaluation tool for myself and my student teachers, and I have watched other teachers use it in class. But what struck me in this instance was the very different way Bill introduced the experience to his class, a very low-key, intuitive, sensitive way that allowed students to experiment with the new medium, independent of and unhindered by any preconceptions on Bill's part as to what they should be doing or what kind of "product" should result. Among the things discovered was that although viewing television is central to young lives, the TV production process is not. Students were amazed to find out that the tapes recorded an image as well as sound and that they didn't have to be "developed" before being played back. Playback was instant, like the rest of their lives. So he let them play with the hardware, learn about lenses and tapes, discover its optical and electronic limitations, and then do with it what they felt like doing, making something of it entirely their own. The entire class became transfixed with the new

technology which he had brought into their midst. Asian students and others who could barely speak English found a new means of expression. Like some personal possession the camera and its recorder was swept about the room, out the door, out into the halls and into other rooms, a magical device for moving through space and time. There was now in their hands a whole new way of gathering information about the school, the neighborhood, the world, and, what's more, they were in control of it! Bill anticipated some of these things; others were a surprise for both of us.

I once asked him why he had brought this new technology into his class and taken a step into the future from which neither he nor his students could ever return . . .

I just knew that it would be a turn-on, but my thinking about it came after the first time I used it. I brought it in just as something to show them, thinking they would play with it for one day or two, but it turned into a long experience, a whole semester. I began to see that it was a way for a whole bunch of different people to talk to others whom they didn't know how to talk to before.

But you had some inkling of what might happen?

I knew that something would happen, I knew that some people would start talking to each other, and I knew that some people would be threatened by it, but I couldn't tell at that time who. The most significant thing that happened was that two

or three girls who usually hang around the side and back of the room, just sitting there, slowly becoming nonentities in the class, just grabbed it, just took it and interviewed everybody in the room and asked them the most real questions, like why are you here and are you having a good time, is it worth it, and questions like that which no one is allowed to ask in the regular framework of the class. This is why I keep bringing it back, because they're asking questions which I think are more valid than the questions I ask.

What was the initial reaction to the appearance of this new technology in the classroom?

It varied. It seems there's a different level of understanding of what TV is. It seems like the white kids really relate to TV differently than black kids. The black kids sort of goofed on it and goofed on the media: There's nothing happening! Schools' dead! They answered pretty realistically from their own feelings, while the white kids tried to manipulate what was going to come out the next day on the TV screen, and they realized that they couldn't and became scared. That made everyone sort of turn away, whereas the black kids could turn right to the TV and rapped right at it. The white kids, because they somehow couldn't really manipulate the image that was going to come out, and thought about it, would turn their heads away and come out with the simplest answer so the interviewer would go away.

But, they really liked it . . .

I think that the most obvious thing was that the day after I brought in the equipment, instead of having 25 people there I had 35 people, people whom I hadn't seen. They had heard about it from their friends, that this was happening, and they could relate to it. So they showed up in class, and all the seats were filled. I knew something was happening . . . I had to go out and find more chairs. And next I noticed some feeling that this was a class, a feeling that hadn't really been there before, and it was short-lived because of a lot of other factors. We were people who shared the experience of being on TV. We could talk about that experience rather than talk about some things that they didn't really share. It was pretty spontaneous. The next day we sat around and watched it, and I remember people telling other people what they had done. There were four or five conversations going on at the same time, which were hard to keep track of. It seemed like it just generated off the film, especially the last part of the film when James was singing.

Then from this initial, happy experience you decided to go on, to do more with it. You and I talked about a TV course, so I know it was already at the back of your mind. Let's talk for a while about what you envision your course to be, how you proposed it to your curriculum committee, and the kinds of problems that arose.

I just see it as process versus product. We're not trying to learn a whole bunch of facts in the course content, but the curriculum committee wouldn't allow a course that didn't have categorized facts. I had to include a lot of things about the study of the history of the media to date in order to make it legitimate, in order that it's social-studies. I included something on the study of the presidents

I knew something was happening
I had to go out and find more chairs

through the media, which is a legitimate thing to study, but I had to include that or they would never have passed the course. What I really teach the course for is to have the kids experience the process of television, and the reason that I like the TV is that it is a major source of information. I took a poll in my class, in all my classes, to find out how much time they were watching television. Their TVs were on an average of 6½ hours a day and they were watching an average of 3 hours and 20 minutes. I doubt if there's any kid at that school who is reading even half that much. And so their source of information, values, and models were through real information, news and television, yet no one was talking about it, no one knew this. I think it's very important to synchronize school and their real environment.

It would seem to me that's a rather elemental fact, that the importance of television in children's lives would be obvious to parents and teachers, and, most of all to the kids themselves. Or is it, as McLuhan says, that we are oblivious to it, as unaware of it as a fish is to the water in which he swims?

The fact that I'm talking about TV they can't understand. A few of them complained to their parents that it wasn't social studies or even a subject to be brought up in school. And that came back to me.

The principal calls me up and says, "Are you talking about television in your classes? Is that social studies?" Yeah . . . you know it's about twenty years old and changing our lives, that's all. It's almost impossible to explain to someone who doesn't understand that history means today too. But they really didn't understand that it was doing anything

at all, because especially for these kids, as opposed to us, it was introduced into our lives after we had already been around—this is part of their environment, and they don't really say, well television is different from anything else, because it's just part of what they experience. But just one day of talking about it does a lot to increase the awareness of what television is doing to them. I know all these kids will go home today, and when they watch television they will relate to that television differently than they did before. I think they'll begin to be able to see—especially if you did it a lot—the manipulative aspects of television—commercials—they're just not spontaneous, no matter how fluid they look, it's not just coincidence that a television is in that guy's bathroom and happens to catch him making a comment about his deodorant . . .

I was really amazed at the way the kids took to the hardware. They weren't frightened by it at all or the least bit hesitant to use it. In fact, what really amazed me was the way the girls took to it; they made it all go, they were the ones who just seemed to pick it up and make things happen in class . . .

The boys almost never act as interviewers. Only when forced into it. They can be part of a production which they had thought up. Like James could sing, but he probably had been thinking about it for fifteen minutes after he had been watching everyone else. The guys, because of age, might really be threatened by anything they couldn't control. But for the girls it was different. There's no control anyway, they thought, so we might as well enjoy it. Or they thought: here's something we can control, and they recognized it quicker.

Any ideas why this happens?

the principal calls me up and says, 'are you talking about television in your classes? Is that social studies?'

I think it's the immediate feedback, because I happen to think that's really important, and that's why it's a new advance in technology. Almost every advance in evolution is that you store information and you put it out. Other animals do it through genetic ways, so it takes generations to change. We have other kinds of information storage and response mechanisms that are really fast, and TV is a really fast storage-retrieval process of information. But that doesn't explain why a girl is holding onto it the first day and she hasn't even seen the playback. Maybe it's because it looks like a tape recorder and a big 16mm camera sitting on someone's shoulders; it's something other people use to make other kinds of things that they can relate to.

Again, there is the message, the medium and the hardware having more impact than the content . . .

That's the reason I like it—it fits my style, and I don't think it fits everybody's style. My style is that I feel they learn more from experiencing the media than they do by getting something done, something that you want to have done before you walk into the class. If they used it for one minute and had only one minute of playback. That's what they experience.

Then you don't anticipate the introduction of videotape into class by making some assignment, somehow structuring from the very beginning how it will be used and related to? Did you introduce it in any way to the class?

I don't think so. I just brought it in one day and it made for much more spontaneity. One of the differences was that I wasn't looking for a product. To introduce the medium I would just bring in the hardware and set it down, teach a couple of kids how to use the camera and tell them how it works, and just let it happen. They'll find something to do with it. As soon as someone really starts getting into it—it's brand new and TV and they like TV— and they're a star, and even if they're nervous and shaky and can't think of the next thing to ask they're still a star and having a pretty good time, so that someone else will get it sooner or later. The lesson is the process and not that they're going to make a commercial—two months from now. What they're going to experience is a TV being there that they can play back and see themselves and use themselves as information. It's not exactly what they do. That's secondary information, for the first time. That's why it will beat filming. That's also why film hasn't caught on. It's too expensive and too long a delay. So if you wait two weeks for the film to come back and you edit it, then you send it back and have that all done to it, then half the term is over. Here you can do it and that's it. You can create something for as long as it takes you to do it.

How long does this period of unstructured, spontaneous experimentation last?

Well the exploratory period can last a pretty long time, I think, and it depends on how uptight I get, vis-a-vis all the other things that are happening in the school. The more I look at it, the more I experience it as really a threat to the working of the school. That's why I really like it. It's an information threat to the school. Now the information, instead of coming from the principal to the assistant principal to me to the kids through the ditto thing every Monday morning, comes from the kids, and *that* is a threat, and I'm understanding it more

It's almost impossible to explain to someone who doesn't understand that history means today too!

129

and more as I use it. In the introductory time there's a lot of things they can do and play with; like they can go out and interview all the different kinds of people in the classroom. When I teach that course the video tape is going to be all around the school, and that undermines the information given out by the school. And that can last a pretty long time. They can get better and better at interviews . . . .

Probably the most successful course in the school is the drama course, and there are many things happening all the time. No one really is in control. The drama teacher is never trying to be in control; she just tries to generate interest to begin with and doesn't have too much of that to do because it's a voluntary course. Everybody gets into it, and that's pretty much what I hope happens. It won't happen totally. It will happen for some of the kids. The kids that can just self-generate I will never see again; it'll become their course. And that would be maybe a fourth of the people. The other people will go around and interview people and not *quite* get on that sophistication and spontaneity that they need, and I would spend a lot of time with them, drilling and looking over the tapes. Instead of having something concrete ready to happen they could trip on the happening, and that could last a long time; that could be an exploratory period that could last three or four weeks.

When you get through the exploratory period, what happens then? What kinds of projects or assignments would you suggest? Would you work toward any particular objectives?

The interview is one. You go out and try to make a product, a film, where any person who didn't know who they were watching would come out knowing something about the person or his position. So they interview the football coach. They could find out a lot about him, about his philosophy of coaching, his teaching, what he's like with the kids. They could interview kids and see what they see in the coach. And we can almost have an encounter session through the media. On film you'll have different opinions about each other, and they can put together a product, taking out the stuff that's irrelevant. By taking out the stuff they think is irrelevant they are making value judgments. So that's what the process is. You begin to make judgments about your life, or about the media, or what is important. If someone says, what do you think about the school, and you say, it's all right; then, how is it all right? If you can generate information from one person then you'll learn a lot about the person. You're learning the technique of that and also the technique of knowing what's wrong.

While watching the monitor this morning one of the girls said something to the effect that television changes the environment, that the room on the screen looks different from the room in reality. She was beginning to grasp the idea that the cameraman has a lot of power, that by choosing a particular lens or a particular angle he can alter the environment and the relationships of all the elements in it. When a student says this, does it suggest to you something of the responsibility a teacher has, the responsibility you have to teach them about this power of the medium, the power to distort?

Sure. If they make a film about a person in the school, they'll have the responsibility of asking themselves, do you think that that's a real vision of

So that's what the process is. You begin to make judgements about your life, or about the media, or what is important.

130

the person? That will be their responsibility, the reporter's responsibility. Can you really go up and ask a person who's just been in a car accident, how do you feel? It might make for a great film, but you're adding to his pain. In your responsibility of trying to be true you have the responsibility of trying to understand what you're trying to be true to; this is basically your value judgment. A lot of the questions from the kids were fairly aggressive, or their reactions to the responses were aggressive. This affects the person being interviewed. As they begin to understand how they're being aggressive and what effect this has, they will become better information gatherers. And that can still be in the exploratory stage before they even begin to look at how to make a product.

This responsibility thing suggests another outcome—their ability to transfer what they've learned in class about the power of the medium to their own understanding of what they see at home during the three or four hours they're in front of the tube. Is this just a byproduct, something they pick up intuitively, or would you plan specific activities that would get across this relationship between the process of shooting a videotape and the process of watching one on a network program?

I think I would do a lot of things like just ask them to pay more attention to it, to keep track of commercials they see on the six o'clock news. Ten kids will come back who've done it. And there will be all this information about aspirin and Bufferin, and something for your stomach, something for your feet, and something for your arthritis; like that's really a great take-off place. Why are all these ads on? What is America that at six o'clock every-

one is vulnerable to Bufferin ads? We had a good discussion the other day off that information. Could you tell just from watching the commercials who was watching TV? So we all sat around and thought: what are the commercials on Saturday morning? There isn't one Bufferin commercial on at nine o'clock Saturday morning; they're all for toys and crispy eaters. Just those kinds of exercises which don't involve any really deep thought in doing generate a lot of input, just because everyone has done something, and they all can relate to TV because they all watch it. A few people, the next time they see a Bufferin ad, they'll think about it, and who is watching it. And after that you say, what are they trying to get me to do and how are they trying to get me to do it? I will go about the same process in getting them to understand those things, like just acting out commercials . . .

One of the outcomes, then, would be their understanding of how advertisers manipulate the viewer—a very subtle thing, particularly when, as you say, you've grown up with it and don't perceive it as being different or wrong. Are there other things they are learning, either through experience with the medium in school or at home?

It's hard to say because partly it's what I've learned. I can tell what I've learned, and it's hard for me to tell what they're learning. The contradiction in their lives is that they accept television as reality. At the same time I'm not sure they accept any of it as reality. They'll watch the Vietnam war and know that that's true, and that it's happening. They'll see a wounded soldier and maybe empathize with his pain; at the same time they don't really empathize at all, because they can just go to school

The contradiction in their lives is that they accept television as reality. At the same time I'm not sure they accept any of it as reality.

131

or just see the guy carried across the screen in pain and then call their friend and ask something totally irrelevant to it. So it's in their house and in their life, but they don't really see it as reality. I think one of the things that will happen is that if they experience television they will begin to tell the difference between a documentary and half an hour of soap opera. I think their differentiation isn't that acute. It's a process that will really be speeded up with the use of equipment.

And while all these things are happening there are all these other kinds of things happening out in the school, among the faculty. Let's come back to the question asked of you by the school curriculum committee—what does all this have to do with social studies? The question is significant, and it's telling; telling of the state of mind of many, perhaps most teachers. Ron Valentine was asked that same question about his course in a different school. Anybody who attempts to do a TV course or who begins to act upon the larger implications of any of the things suggested in this book are going to encounter that question or response to what we're doing . . .

At one level that is a fear response. Stop it, 'cause I don't understand it! It's not social studies! In the curriculum committee a person said to me, that's not social studies, that's English! My visceral response was, who cares! There's no difference. It's all happening, it's all around us. This idea that you can't read a poem in your social studies class or have them write a poem in a social studies class, or have them write at all—I don't classify that way. And one of the people who voted against the course wasn't a social studies person but an English teacher who thought it should have been an English class. They're threatened by it; the first problem is they don't understand what it is and then they try to dissect it and put it into a compartment. And it doesn't really fit a compartment, so I have to add things that they can compartmentalize. They can easily show a film that I made, but they wouldn't know how to let the kids make a film. There's a generation gap in this teacher body based upon those who can't understand the medium and those who can.

I'll have to admit, though, that there are aspects of TV that bother me too. Like today I was watching the kids as they viewed the playback of the tape they made yesterday, and I became conscious of the looks on their faces, the intensity with which they watched that lighted screen, an intensity that I don't see when I'm talking to them, that you don't see when they're reading a book or even when they're watching a movie. It's scary. It bothers me that they seem to be relating to that machine in a more comfortable, well, at least a more direct way—I don't know if it's more comfortable—a more intense way than they can relate to human beings. And isn't that bad? Are you helping them to relate to machines at the cost of real human relationships? Or are we helping them to deal with the inevitable, a life of working with, talking to, living with machines? I don't know, but I feel uneasy about it.

I'm not really sure. I appreciate intensity. My positive response is intensity isn't a bad thing. It can be transferred from one form to another. If you generate intensity, even if it's with a machine, it will overlap into the next conversation. Energy overlaps. My negative response is, *Stop doing it*

and next I noticed some feeling that this was a class, a feeling that hadn't really been there before

immediately!

But machines make us lazy. The television technique being selective, selecting for us what we will see—won't that make us lazy? We'll cease to be observant, perceptive, questioning with our eyes; we'll just take what comes along. It can be crippling in a way . . .

At the same time, if you're holding onto the camera, then you have to decide what to select and you become aware of that selection, which is also what you become aware of when you focus your eyes. You may not be aware; you just do it. It's a conscious thing when you decide what you're going to watch through the camera. That's good for one person and for the other thirty people who get to watch.

I know you don't watch much television, in fact you don't even have a television set . . .

Yeah, I have a television set.

You have a television set. But it's not obvious, it's not around . . . do you spend much time watching it?

One of the bad spin-offs of the course is that now I've started watching TV. You know, not like John Lennon, I don't leave it on as a fireplace, but I've started watching it and saying to myself, how would I use that commercial in class? instead of watching it as information. I really don't like commercial television very much. I see it as symbolic of America, everything that has gone wrong with America—its crass commercialism, everything. I really don't like watching the symbols of the worst part of America . . .

It intrudes on us. I'm trying to avoid all that shit, and I don't want it in my house . . .

I think that's one of the things that might, at a sophisticated level, be taught through a television course, that you're letting that in your house and it's affecting you, and I use it as a way of talking about life, talking about how I live to the kids. About the fact that I don't buy what they're selling on TV. I use my money for something else. It's a way of generating interaction. And that interaction is pretty good because I think in most schools there's almost no interaction, no interaction in class—there's a lot of interaction for five minutes here and there in the halls. The hall is the kids' room. The teachers each have one room, but the kids share one l-o-n-g room, and they're allowed to be in the hall for five minutes. After five minutes I'm sorry, you need a pass. I really think that interaction is like the seed. I think the American isolation is that people can't somehow tell each other what's really happening in their lives . . .

I remember we had a workshop a couple of years ago, the idea being that we'd sit down and brainstorm the problem of low reading scores. And I remember how it struck me, because I was getting there too. Here we sit worrying about whether or not kids can read well, and they're watching television. I mean, it reminds me of the year 1450; Gutenberg has just perfected a printing process, and the faculty of Old Heidelberg High are sitting around worrying about why fewer kids are going into "Scribe 101" when in fact they ought to be thinking about a printing class. The kids have found a new medium; hell, they really know no other, it's been around all their lives. We bought it for them—parents I mean— we brought it into the house; we introduced kids to the damned thing and now we've got to take on the responsibility of showing them how to use it, or

we had shared the experience of being on TV

133

*learn from them. Maybe we ought to be concerned
with facilitating, improving their perceptions of
visual media. But how are we to bridge the now and
the future? I'm sure this is part of what you're up
against with this new TV course. What do you tell
people when they're concerned about the now, and
the future is crashing in on us faster than we know?*

I always talk about this to someone like you who
I know can understand what I'm saying. I've never
talked about this to someone who doesn't understand, because he'll start asking me how I'm going
to evaluate the students and we'll end up trying to
figure out which product we're going to make in
my class. He'll begin to say, what type is that? Is
it a Sony? Is that a Panasonic? It's like, what kind
of car do you drive? Rather than I drive or I drove
there—I *went* there. Or, that was sure a nice tree I
drove by. I don't really know what to say to them.
One of the things I started saying to people, and
it's hard for me not to say it aggressively, is that for
a long time people would look at the future and
see nothing but a greater past, more and more of
the past, more and more being better and better.
No one really thinks that the future is going to be
different. But there's not going to be a bigger past;
there's going to be a different future. And I think
that that happens maybe two or three times in a
generation. If someone looked out their window
only three times in their life and saw downtown
Oakland, they would see three views that would
be totally different, not just a little bit more of
the same thing. That's like future shock to me.
Bigger and bigger airplanes I can dig, but a totally
different way of communicating through space,
through extra-sensory perception to someone

else—it freaks me out. It scares me. I'm frightened
by it. It makes me nervous. People are telling me
about ESP, and I'm tantalized by it; I want to hear
about it, but at the same time this little queasiness
happens in my stomach, because it's really different.
That will be here in the future, and some people are
already doing it. And when I try to explain that to
someone . . .

I've tried to explain it to one of the teachers,
and the look on his face was: Who let this man in
here? I could just see him reporting me to someone,
to some authority who would make sure the future
wasn't different because he'd stop me.

*I think the American isolation is that people can't
somehow tell each other what's really happening in their lives.*

To: Bill Ames

Fr: MG, vice principal

The desk tops in your classroom were scrubbed by the Saturday
detention crew. Please keep them unmarred. YOUR HOUSEKEEPING
IS DISGRACEFUL Bill. Will you please get things straightened up
immediately and insist that your students restore order daily.

What is the purpose of the mattress? (I would like an answer) Those
beat up couches should go immediately (I'll bring it to the attention
of Frank that I told you to get rid of them and he can discuss with
you whether I am right or wrong.)

I will be by Wednesday to see the condition of your room.

cc: FW, principal

P. S. If that carpet is to stay, it must be cleaned and kept cleaned
by you or your classes.

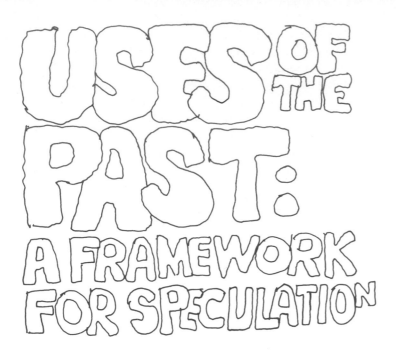

USES OF THE PAST: A FRAMEWORK FOR SPECULATION

Herman Kahn is an historian with a sense of the past and the future, though his too-real book *On Thermonuclear War* and his computation of death's exponent are acts for which many still deny him forgiveness. Nevertheless, he is part of a small group of visionaries like Buckminster Fuller, Daniel Bell, Alvin Toffler, Marshall McLuhan, and others, who see environments as they really are, who seem to be in touch with the essences of both the past and the future, and who, like their counterparts in every age before them, are considered by some to be very perceptive and by others to be very insane. The value of *The Year 2000* for teachers is its pragmatic approach and the accessibility of the authors' minds to the reader. Kahn and Wiener begin with some reasons for studying the future, including predicting future conditions and the outcomes of current.trends and policies; anticipating problems early enough to plan effectively for their eventuality; and the related problems of establishing priorities and timing in government programs, for example, or, as we might infer, in education. What is significant is the authors' recognition that while the future is indeed impossible to predict with great accuracy, reading about it, teaching about it, and discussing it in the classroom can broaden students' understanding and encourage creative approaches to consideration of future problems and opportunities, while at the same time altering basic beliefs, assumptions, and patterns of behavior such as students' feelings about ambivalence, uncertainty, and the myth of stability. The methods developed by the authors are explicit throughout. Not only do their findings suggest alternatives for the content of a course which would prepare children and teachers to live in the future, but, more helpful, (for content changes faster than we can grasp its presence or its implications) they suggest a framework and several strategies—surprise-free projections, analysis of trends, and the construction of scenarios for the future—for now and for future courses. But how does one remember things before they happen? Kahn and Weiner explain one way . . .

In this study we have used several interrelated devices to facilitate making systematic conjectures about the future. The most important, of course, is simply to think about the problem—to seek to identify important long-term trends which seem likely to continue. These trends include the world-wide spread of a more or less secular humanism, the institutionalization of scientific and technological innovation, the expectation of continuous economic growth, and the like. For our purposes we have identified a complex, long-term "multifold trend" consisting of thirteen interrelated elements.

In addition, we have considered how the problem of projecting one-third century ahead might have appeared in 1933, 1900, and so on, in order to get a sense of the current and future pace of change and the likelihood of unexpected developments, and to identify significant clusters of events, qualitative changes in the combination of trends, and emergent properties, such as the increasing self-consciousness of time and history.

Next we have attempted to construct significant baselines, statistical where possible, to project key variables in society. These include population, literacy, gross national product, energy sources, military strength, and the like; these variables and their growth rates tend both to furnish and to constrain the possibilities for any society. By selecting extrapolations of current or emerging tendencies that grow continuously out of today's world and reflect the multifold trend and our current expectations, we create a "surprise-free" projection—one that seems less surprising than any other specific possibility. Consistent with this projection, we describe a "standard world".

(1) What will the world be like in the year 2000?
(2) How old will your students be then? And how old will you be?
(3) What kinds of skills and understandings will be required to live in such a world?

After this point the book becomes a maze of charts, tables, graphs, and scenarios quite literally projecting the reader to the year 2000. All of which suggests what the content, the emphasis, and the strategies of courses preparing students for the future might be . . .

137

There Is a Basic, Long-Term Multifold Trend Toward:

1. Increasingly Sensate (empirical, this-worldly, secular, humanistic, pragmatic, utilitarian, contractual, epicurean or hedonistic, and the like) cultures
2. Bourgeois, bureaucratic, "meritocratic," democratic (and nationalistic?) elites
3. Accumulation of scientific and technological knowledge
4. Institutionalization of change, especially research, development, innovation, and diffusion
5. Worldwide industrialization and modernization
6. Increasing affluence and (recently) leisure
7. Population growth
8. Urbanization and (soon) the growth of megalopolises
9. Decreasing importance of primary and (recently) secondary occupations
10. Literacy and education
11. Increasing capability for mass destruction
12. Increasing tempo of change
13. Increasing universality of the multifold trend

Some Perspectives on Change

A second way of looking at the future is to identify the relevant clusters of events that have marked off different time periods in man's history. One can thus seek to identify the constants of each time, the secular trend lines, and the "turning points" of an era. For our purpose we begin by considering what a "surprise-free" projection might have been like in 1900 or 1933.

Year 1900

One world (Western-dominated), though with many unassimilated, traditional cultures
Industrial, colonial, or "protected" societies
Declining United Kingdom and France—rising Germany, United States, Russia, and Japan
Parliamentary government and Christianity
Basic feeling in almost all classes of the white race (and in many non-white) of optimism, security, progress, order, and physical supremacy of Western culture, and a belief in rational and moral domestic and foreign politics, and perhaps most important of all, a relative absence of guilt feelings
Intellectual acceptance of the ideas of Adam Smith, Darwin, and the Enlightenment by the West

First Third of the Twentieth Century

Russo-Japanese War
"La Belle Epoque" (1901-1913)
Mexican (1910) and Chinese (1911) social (and racial) revolutions
World War I—Europe partly devastated
Five major dynasties (Hohenzollern, Hapsburg, Romanov, Manchu, and Ottoman) dethroned
Emergence of United States as leading world power
Loss of European (and democratic) morale and prestige
Rise of Communism and Soviet Union
Great Depression
Rise of Fascist ideologies and diverse dictatorships
Upsetting impact of new intellectual concepts, such as those of Bohr, de Broglie, Einstein, Freud, and Schroedinger

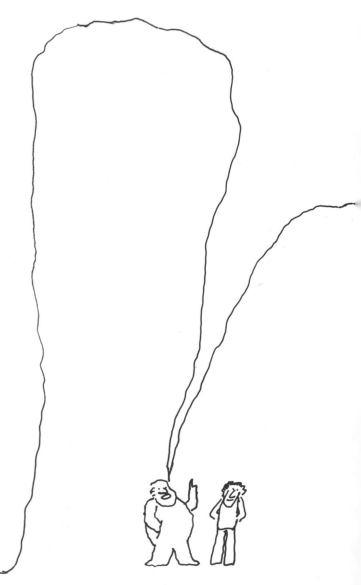

138

Second Third of the Twentieth Century

Continued growth of Communism and Fascism

World War II—Europe again devastated

Mass murder and forced population movements on extraordinary scale before, during, and after World War II

Intense, nationalistic competition in the development and application of radically new technologies for both peace and war

Decolonization

The Cold War and Neutralism

Shifts in power position

    Rise and decline of Italy, Canada, and India

    Decline and reemergence of Europe

    Decline and reemergence of Japan

    Reunification and centralization of China

    Emergence of

        Two super powers (U.S. and S.U.)

        Five large powers (Japan, W. Germany, France, China, U.K.)

        Three intermediate powers (India, Italy, Canada)

Post-Keynesian, post-Marxian, and perhaps post-communal and sophisticated "development" economics

Emergence of mass-consumption societies

"Second" wave of industrial revolutions

Chinese achieve nuclear status

Final Third of the Twentieth Century
(Relatively Apolitical and Surprise-Free Projection)

1. Continuation of basic, long-term "multifold trend"
2. Emergence of "postindustrial" culture
3. Worldwide capability for modern technology
4. Very small world: increasing need for regional or worldwide "zoning ordinances" for control of arms, technology, pollution, trade, transportation, population, resource utilization, and the like
5. High (1 to 10 per cent) growth rates in GNP per capita
6. Increasing emphasis on "meaning and purpose"
7. Much turmoil in the "new" and possibly in the industrializing nations
8. Some possibility for sustained "natavist," messianic, or other mass movements
9. Second rise of Japan (to being potentially, nominally, or perhaps actually, the third largest power)
10. Some further rise of Europe and China
11. Emergence of new intermediate powers, such as Brazil, Mexico, Pakistan, Indonesia, East Germany, and Egypt
12. Some decline (relative) of the U.S. and the U.S.S.R.
13. A possible absence of stark "life and death" political and economic issues in the old nations

*A Relatively "Surprise-Free" Early
Twenty-First Century*

1. We expect the rise of new great powers—perhaps Japan, China, a European complex, Brazil, Mexico, or India.

2. There will be new political, perhaps even "philosophical," issues.

3. There will be a leveling off or diminishing of some aspects of the basic, long-term multifold trend, such as urbanization.

4. The postindustrial and industrial worlds will have been largely realized.

5. Some success seems likely with population control, arms control, and some kind of moderately stable international security arrangements, though probably not a "world government."

6. In the industrializing world, disorder, ideology, and irrational movements will probably continue to play disruptive though geographically confined roles.

7. In the U.S. and Western Europe, there will presumably be either a return to certain Hellenic or older European concépts of the good life, or an intensified alienation and search for identity, values, meaning, and purpose, a search made necessary and facilitated by the unprecedented affluence and permissiveness of the postindustrial economy.

ONE HUNDRED TECHNICAL INNOVATIONS VERY LIKELY IN THE LAST THIRD OF THE TWENTIETH CENTURY (COUNT 'EM, ONE HUNDRED)

1. Multiple applications of lasers and masers for sensing, measuring, communication, cutting, heating, welding, power transmission, illumination, destructive (defensive), and other purposes.
2. Extreme high-strength and/or high-temperature structural materials
3. New or improved superperformance fabrics (papers, fibers, and plastics)
4. New or improved materials for equipment and appliances (plastics, glasses, alloys, ceramics, intermetallics, and cements)
5. New airborne vehicles (ground-effect machines, VTOL and STOL, super-helicopters, giant and/or supersonic jets)
6. Extensive commercial application of shaped-charge explosives
7. More reliable and longer-range weather forecasting
8. Intensive and/or extensive expansion of tropical agriculture and forestry
9. New sources of power for fixed installations (e.g., magnetohydrodynamic, thermionic and thermoelectric, and radioactivity)
10. New sources of power for ground transportation (storage battery, fuel cell, propulsion [or support] by electro-magnetic fields, jet engine, turbine, and the like)
11. Extensive and intensive worldwide use of high altitude cameras for mapping, prospecting, census, land use, and geological investigations
12. New methods of water transportation (such as large submarines, flexible and special purpose "container ships," or more extensive use of large automated single-purpose bulk cargo ships)
13. Major reduction in hereditary and congenital defects
14. Extensive use of cyborg techniques (mechanical aids or substitutes for human organs, senses, limbs, or other components)
15. New techniques for preserving or improving the environment
16. Relatively effective appetite and weight control
17. New techniques and institutions for adult education
18. New and useful plant and animal species
19. Human "hibernation" for short periods (hours or days) for medical purposes
20. Inexpensive design and procurement of "one of a kind" items through use of computerized analysis and automated production
21. Controlled and/or supereffective relaxation and sleep
22. More sophisticated architectural engineering (e.g., geodesic domes, "fancy" stressed shells, pressurized skins, and esoteric materials)
23. New or improved uses of the oceans (mining, extraction of minerals, controlled "farming," source of energy, and the like)
24. Three-dimensional photography, illustrations, movies, and television

"DEAR, SUPPER'S READY!"

25. Automated or more mechanized housekeeping and home maintenance
26. Widespread use of nuclear reactors for power
27. Use of nuclear explosives for excavation and mining, generation of power, creation of high temperature—high-pressure environments, and/or as a source of neutrons or other radiation
28. General use of automation and cybernation in management and production
29. Extensive and intensive centralization (or automatic interconnection) of current and past personal and business information in high-speed data processors
30. Other new and possibly pervasive techniques for surveillance, monitoring, and control of individuals and organizations
31. Some control of weather and/or climate
32. Other (permanent or temporary) changes—or experiments—with the overall environment (e.g., the "permanent" increase in C-14 and temporary creation of other radioactivity by nuclear explosions, the increasing generation of CO_2 in the atmosphere, projects Starfire, West Ford, and Storm Fury)
33. New and more reliable "educational" and propaganda techniques for affecting human behavior—public and private
34. Practical use of direct electronic communication with and stimulation of the brain
35. Human hibernation for relatively extensive periods (months to years)
36. Cheap and widely available central war weapons and weapon systems
37. New and relatively effective counterinsurgency techniques (and perhaps also insurgency techniques)

38. New techniques for very cheap, convenient, and reliable birth control
39. New, more varied, and more reliable drugs for control of fatigue, relaxation, alertness, mood, personality, perceptions, fantasies, and other psychobiological states
40. Capability to choose the sex of unborn children
41. Improved capability to "change" sex of children and/or adults
42. Other genetic control and/or influence over the "basic constitution" of an individual
43. New techniques and institutions for the education of children
44. General and substantial increase in life expectancy, postponement of aging, and limited rejuvenation
45. Generally acceptable and competitive synthetic foods and beverages (e.g., carbohydrates, fats, proteins, enzymes, vitamins, coffee, tea, cocoa, and alcoholic liquor)
46. "High quality" medical care for undeveloped areas (e.g., use of medical aides and technicians, referral hospitals, broad spectrum antibiotics, and artificial blood plasma)

47. Design and extensive use of responsive and supercontrolled environments for private and public use (for pleasurable, educational, and vocational purposes)

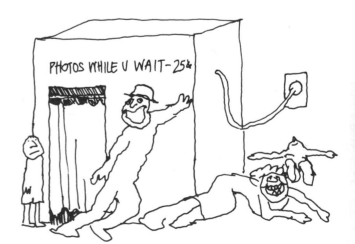

PHOTOS WHILE U WAIT—25¢

48. Physically nonharmful methods of overindulging

49. Simple techniques for extensive and "permanent" cosmetological changes (features, "figures," perhaps complexion and even skin color, and even physique)

50. More extensive use of transplantation of human organs

51. Permanent manned satellite and lunar installations—interplanetary travel

52. Application of space life systems or similar techniques to terrestrial installations

53. Permanent inhabited undersea installations and perhaps even colonies

54. Automated grocery and department stores

55. Extensive use of robots and machines "slaved" to humans

56. New use of underground "tunnels" for private and public transportation and other purposes

57. Automated universal (real time) credit, audit and banking systems

58. Chemical methods for improving memory and learning

59. Greater use of underground buildings

60. New and improved materials and equipment for buildings and interiors (e.g., variable transmission glass, heating and cooling by thermoelectric effect, and electroluminescent and phosphorescent lighting)

61. Widespread use of cryogenics

62. Improved chemical control of some mental illnesses and some aspects of senility

63. Mechanical and chemical methods for improving human analytical ability more or less directly

64. Inexpensive and rapid techniques for making tunnels and underground cavities in earth and/or rock

65. Major improvements in earth moving and construction equipment generally

66. New techniques for keeping physically fit and/or acquiring physical skills

67. Commercial extraction of oil from shale

68. Recoverable boosters for economic space launching

69. Individual flying platforms

70. Simple inexpensive home video recording and playing

71. Inexpensive high-capacity, worldwide, regional, and local (home and business) communication (perhaps using satellites, lasers, and light pipes)

72. Practical home and business use of "wired" video communication for both telephone and TV (possibly including retrieval of taped material from libraries or other sources) and rapid transmission and reception of facsimilies (possibly including news, library material, commercial announcements, instantaneous mail delivery, other printouts, and so on)

73. Practical large-scale desalinization

74. Pervasive business use of computers for the storage, processing, and retrieval of information

75. Shared time (public and interconnected?) computers generally available to home and business on a metered basis

76. Other widespread use of computers for intellectual and professional assistance (translation, teaching, literature search, medical diagnosis, traffic control, crime detection, computation, design, analysis and to some degree as intellectual collaborator generally)

77. General availability of inexpensive transuranic and other esoteric elements

78. Space defense systems

79. Inexpensive and reasonably effective ground-based BMD

80. Very low-cost buildings for home and business use

81. Personal "pagers" (perhaps even two-way pocket phones) and other personal electronic equipment for communication, computing, and data processing program

82. Direct broadcasts from satellites to home receivers

83. Inexpensive (less than $20), long lasting, very small battery operated TV receivers

84. Home computers to "run" household and communicate with outside world

85. Maintenance-free, longlife electronic and other equipment

86. Home education via video and computerized and programmed learning

87. Stimulated and planned and perhaps programmed dreams

88. Inexpensive (less than one cent a page), rapid high-quality black and white reproduction; followed by color and high-detailed photography reproduction—perhaps for home as well as office use

89. Widespread use of improved fluid amplifiers

90. Conference TV (both closed circuit and public communication system)

91. Flexible penology without necessarily using prisons (by use of modern methods of surveillance, monitoring, and control)

92. Common use of (longlived?) individual power source for lights, appliances, and machines

93. Inexpensive worldwide transportation of humans and cargo

94. Inexpensive road-free (and facility-free) transportation

95. New methods for rapid language teaching

96. Extensive genetic control for plants and animals

97. New biological and chemical methods to identify, trace, incapacitate, or annoy people for police and military uses

98. New and possibly very simple methods for lethal biological and chemical warfare

99. Artificial moons and other methods for lighting large areas at night

100. Extensive use of "biological processes" in the extraction and processing of minerals

The following are areas in which technological success by the year 2000 seems substantially less likely (even money bets, give or take a factor of five), but where, if it occurred, it would be quite important, are these:

Some Less Likely but Important Possibilities

1. "True" artificial intelligence
2. Practical use of sustained fusion to produce neutrons and/or energy
3. Artificial growth of new limbs and organs (either in situ or for late transplantation)
4. Room temperature superconductors
5. Major use of rockets for commercial or private transportation (either terrestrial or extraterrestrial)
6. Effective chemical or biological treatment for most mental illnesses
7. Almost complete control of marginal changes in heredity
8. Suspended animation (for years or centuries)
9. Practical materials with nearly "theoretical limit" strength
10. Conversion of mammals (humans?) to fluid breathers
11. Direct input into human memory banks
12. Direct augmentation of human mental capacity by the mechanical or electrical interconnection of the brain with a computer
13. Major rejuvenation and/or significant extension of vigor and life span—say 100 to 150 years
14. Chemical or biological control of character or intelligence
15. Automated highways
16. Extensive use of moving sidewalks for local transportation
17. Substantial manned lunar or planetary installations
18. Electric power available for less than .3 mill per kilowatt hour
19. Verification of some extrasensory phenomena
20. Planetary engineering
21. Modification of the solar system
22. Practical laboratory conception and nurturing of animal (human?) foetuses
23. Production of a drug equivalent to Huxley's soma
24. A technological equivalent of telepathy
25. Some direct control of individual thought processes

145

We list below ten radical possibilities, some of which hardly make sense. We do not believe that any of them will occur by the year 2000, or perhaps ever. But some of them are discussed today; and such a list does emphasize the fact that some dramatic and radical innovation must be expected. The list may suggest how surprising and exciting (or outrageous) such an event might prove.

Ten Far-Out Possibilities

1. Life expectancy extended to substantially more than 150 years (immortality?)
2. Almost complete genetic control (but still homo sapiens)
3. Major modifications of human species (no longer homo sapiens)
4. Antigravity (or practical use of gravity waves)*
5. Interstellar travel
6. Electric power available for less than .03 mill per kw hour
7. Practical and routine use of extrasensory phenomena
8. Laboratory creation of artificial live plants and animals
9. Lifetime immunization against practically all diseases
10. Substantial lunar or planetary bases or colonies

*As usually envisaged this would make possible a perpetual motion machine and therefore the creation of energy out of nothing. We do not envisage this as even a far-out possibility, but include antigravity, even though it annoys some physicist friends, as an example of some totally new use of a basic phenomena or the seeming violation of a basic law.

And finally there is the possibility — more far-fetched than popular science fiction would have it, but impossible to exclude — of a discovery of extraterrestrial life; or, much more extreme, of communication with extraterrestrial intelligence.

"I can't believe *that!*" said Alice.

"Can't you?" the Queen said in a pitying tone. "Try again; draw a long breath, and shut your eyes."

Alice laughed. "There's no use trying," she said; "one *can't* believe impossible things."

"I dare say you haven't had much practice," said the Queen. "When I was your age I always did it for half an hour a day. Why, sometimes I've believed as many as six impossible things before breakfast!"

EGGS & PEANUT BUTTER

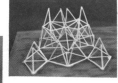

Out behind the school is one of those ubiquitous "portables," the paint flaking off its wood siding, its old space heater not quite up to the cold and damp of the Oakland winter, recalling a time before the memory of any of us there now. But it's an anachronism which, like those stands in the University of Chicago football stadium or the old bicycle shop in Dayton, is an interface between now and the future, one of those unlikely places where things happen. Once inside this weather-beaten time machine one encounters students braver than most, those who are willing to make that quantum leap from the known and secure to the unknown and challenging. They are sprawled on the floor, cutting panels of cardboard for experimental structures, boats, and full-size versions of the balsa wood and paper models of geodesic domes which stand about. Hanging from the ceiling are futuristic egg-carrying vehicles, kites, a paper canoe. The giant canopy of a parachute hovers about your head, and on the board are the scrawled words "NEON MEAT DREAMS." The course taught in this room is called "The Future," but the scene and the action are anything but unwordly; it's all as real as the guy who lives here five days a week with his students. Ron Valentine is no tarot-dealing merlin but one of the most realistic, perceptive, and sensitive people I've ever known. What he teaches is not the "elective frill" many of the faculty imagine it to be, but the stuff of the future, the essence of survival in the very uncertain world to come, the world of Herman Kahn, Buckminster Fuller, and Marshall McLuhan. It's one of the few places in school I enjoy being, one of the few places where some of us feel comfortable.

Sitting with Ron and one of the students in the class, James Korning, we talked about some of the projects that form the core of the semester experience. I began by asking Ron and James how the first problem, building a kite, was presented to the class . . . .

I think I said, well, let's build kites, or why not

148

and suddenly a whole lot of information began to generate on kites. We discovered there's a guy over here who was teaching a kite sculpture class, and he came over and talked about kites. We discovered that there was a lot of incidental trivia on kites and, like, wasn't it the Chinese or Japanese . . .

Oh yeah, they would tie somebody to a kite and send them up there and rather than kill them, put them on the rack, or something like that they would scare the dickens out of them by leaving them up there for a day . . .

The Tibetan monks did that for kicks. That was one of their highs; they just flew up in a kite. The thing was there was such a poverty . . . . it seemed that in everybody's day here at Tech there was such a poverty of anything that somehow or other wasn't justified by getting a job, or in terms of success, or graduating, or getting grades, that this was a welcome relief to the senses. I don't think anybody ever made me defend the idea except for the P.E. coach, who said, well, you know, what do kites got to do with social studies? And we replied what does softball got to do with P.E.? And the only thing I recall is that when the kites were being flown other people outside the class were upset and confused.

The other assignment was this structures thing— with toothpicks and glue build a structure that would support as much weight as you could design it for.

You were limited to a box of toothpicks and some glue, and then there were basic rules. It had to be able to span . . . I've forgotten what we said. Just so you wouldn't take a box of toothpicks and a quart of glue . . .

I think it had to span something like four inches or six inches, but most of the structures were not more than four inches around anyway.

Some of the things we did in class, because maybe it was too difficult to explain them to the rest of the school, to get the rest of the school involved. Other things we made all-school, like the kite contest was an all-school project, and the paper airplane contest.

Given groups within classes that don't talk to each other very much, somehow or other paper airplanes provide a common denominator, a common problem. You get some of the most bugaloo people in the world, who you would assume would think it was totally uncool to do that, who somehow or other you find out were paper airplane champs in kindergarten or they were the West Oakland top-

spinning champion and that's the last success they had. Then they make a paper airplane, and that's their next success. They fly; there were almost none that didn't fly.

How many kids responded to the paper airplane contest?

The whole class, this room was filled with paper airplanes; it was dangerous during the test-flight period. They were going all over the place.

It was the first time anybody had offered the First Annual Open Oakland Technical High School Kite Flying Contest, so we got Lorraine, who spent two hours every morning getting dressed and came in every day with a new ensemble and then sat for a whole day with that new ensemble and did nothing but sit and stand in the hall. She was the First Annual Open Oakland Tech Kite Flying Queen. She loved posing in her ensemble with the kite. Her mother came, and she came in a super new outfit to the actual contest. The sort of show-biz aspects of it can do a lot of things. We found an ally in Al Prince, who teaches the special education kids. Al Prince got students involved in making the things and a couple of his students actually won the high flying thing, even though the kites they made were questionable. And then, with the toothpick thing, the math department kind of got themselves involved and actually gave credit to the students who constructed the toothpick structures.

Jack Morrison made that an assignment. His classes had to build a bridge with a certain kind of roadway out of so many toothpicks. I don't think too many of the students actually did it.

So the thing actually had some impact on other classes . . .

Yeah, and if you could somehow or other keep generating these ideas I think that it would eventually affect the whole school. It's upsetting to the school, but it's upsetting in a healthy way. You don't have any reference points here other than what you're given and maybe what the students have over cigarettes on the front lawn or something. They have reference points, but there's a totally unreal aspect to this place; and maybe that's part of the problem. Students can't adjust what they know is real to the unreality of what they're being told here. And something as loony and absurd, at least on the surface, as a kite flying contest is a reference point. If you could keep generating those things, that would be a reference point for everyone. With the paper boat contest we involved everyone; we involved Morrison in the science department; he volunteered and we designated him the judge of whether or not they met specifications.

We made him the official tech inspector.

Yeah, and Ruth Eggold, the librarian, displayed all the boats in the library, which was an inconvenience, and the swimming coach allowed them to be floated in his pool, which really pissed him off when he saw all the crap floating around. It was very clean an hour or so later and he was less worried about it. When we had the egg drop thing Pete Cattita helped us.

He had a real flare for it; he loved it. We made official badges, and I think it brought out the best in him.

Tell me how you approach teachers to help.

Didn't we have students . . . ?

Yeah, that was one thing about all the contests, that even the students who weren't building things you managed very neatly to delegate into seeing somebody, to get things done, and there was probably a bunch of students you sent over there who could say, hey, teach, would you be willing to do this? Yeah, we had shop teachers who were judges of it too. The students would go out and make their contacts with people. If a student went to the principal and said, can we fly airplanes off the roof? he would immediately say, oh sure, I don't see why not. And then you would say, o.k. can we have the key? Then it was too late for him to say no.

In other words, everybody had a role, and the students were the ones who approached the least approachable people and were obviously successful, because those people weren't least approachable to them. Because of the dynamics, you or I, or teachers involved with each other, obviously wouldn't get the responses that the students would. All you keep doing is sort of injecting show-biz absurdities into the thing and letting them sort of solve it. The most patriotic kite which the principal closed with was the one that said "Fuck Communism," which sort of got dragged along the ground. Then we made a movie of it and showed it to Miller. Bill thought it was funny . . . and said, "For god's sake don't show this to anyone else . . ."

Then you assigned the egg thing. What was the assignment specifically?

It sort of evolved. That was the culmination of a whole thing we did on eggs. The idea was to take something commonplace, for whatever reason it was commonplace, and then we began gathering facts. We composed an enormous list of little-known facts about eggs—I found two more this weekend. Once you get onto eggs, once you develop the cult of the egg, there's just no end of it. The decorative motif around all Tech doors is from the house of the Medici, which is the egg and the spear, so that eggs are all around Oakland Tech. Then how to tell a hard boiled egg from a fresh egg without breaking it open. The one I found out this weekend: if you put an egg in a glass of water, a fresh egg will sink to the bottom and lay on its side. The less than fresh egg will tend to float. Everybody began gathering these things, and we had people saying, well, my mamma says . . . and they'd go home and they'd talk about this loony goddamn stuff they were doing about eggs and their mammas would say, Well I remember we used to hold a hard-boiled egg in a rag on a bruise and it will draw out the poison and it will make the bruise go away. We were getting all this folklore from down home, folklore on eggs. And this one kid, who hadn't done much of anything, showed us how if you soaked an egg in vinegar it would bounce like a rubber ball, and it did. Up to four feet it bounced pretty good.

By the time we got to the egg-drop contest—you had generated so much momentum after having two contests and we had just come down from the boat contest—we had to think of something just to keep the class from going to pieces.

We made up a ditto. We discussed the rules—what should be legitimate and what shouldn't. We determined that it had to be a vehicle and that it had to drop from the top of the building, roughly three floors, to the grass. We debated whether it should fall on the grass or cement, and then we talked about parachutes, whether that should be permitted . . . How did we get the rules for that?

I don't know. It was after a couple of days of hacking; I think you probably asked Morrison . . . I don't remember, you just said no parachutes. We worked out what would be fair, we looked for loopholes, people would keep saying, but what if . . . you couldn't, like, just get a cardboard box, fill it with foam and stick an egg in it. If you used a box, you had to make it yourself, even if you had to cut out the cardboard yourself.

Were there limitations as to what kind of materials you could use?

No, because James used peanut butter. You made a box that was like a goddamn safe to begin with, filled it with peanut butter with the egg in the center. His problem was that in order to avoid cheating on the egg you had to use the official egg.

152

I remember that. He gave us an egg to carry with us all day. He says, meet me before school and I'll give you guys all eggs. My girl friend and I discovered that if you roll an egg out on the cliff up by the College of Arts and Crafts . . .

It will break.

First of all it will break, yeah, and the yolk will descend by the wayside and the empty shell will continue to tumble on down the hill. And that wasn't really learned on purpose but . . .

The idea was that if you carry around an egg for a whole day you would experience more eggness. Aerodynamically too, you know, the shape of the egg, aesthetically and as a container, there couldn't be a better design than the egg shape.

James, this clicked with you, right?

Well, no it didn't, at least not at first, because by then I was actually sort of getting tired of the contest, and I was raring to go and get into another one. But I was also thinking. My girl friend and I were over at her sister and brother-in-law's house, and we told him about this contest and of course they knew about the boat contest. And he says, you know, I read in the paper somewhere about this professor at Cal who assigned all his students to send him an egg in the mail, and of course, you know what packages in the mail go through. And they said one of the surviving eggs was packed in peanut butter, and I had been toying with the idea of packing it in something like that. Well, Valentine was pushing the self-destructive vehicle, where you throw it out and it destroys itself in the process of saving the egg. I was trying to think of something to pack the egg in where you could use it over and over and where it would be like packing a water balloon in water—you know, the balloon won't break as long as the structure that's holding the water around it doesn't. So peanut butter seemed like the easiest, simplest solution to that.

Why did you choose peanut butter?

Well because he suggested it; it had the right consistency and was easy to work with. We went and got a pound and dumped it into a plastic garbage bag, and that was a wasted $1.39 worth of peanut butter.

Wouldn't something else like jello work?

Yeah, I was thinking of jello. I was trying to think of some kind of medium that we could suspend the egg in. And the more density, the thicker, the better. I was even toying with the idea of casting it in cement or plaster or something, except that you would probably have to destroy the plaster and probably the egg in the process of getting it open to see if it was broken or not.

So you had gotten it down to a point where you figured that the container wasn't really as important as the medium of suspension.

Well, Valentine accused me later of using a Russian overkill-type method—on account of my Russian heritage. I thought there was a possible chance we might have some sort of eliminations where the doggone thing might have to be used again, and I wanted something that would last long after everybody else had smashed theirs to bits. Also I was figuring that we could check it out on the cement. We could have chucked ours off the Kaiser Building on the cement and I bet the egg wouldn't have broken.

In your opinion, what was the most elegant design?

Mine. It was elegantly designed and badly flown, because I forgot to put a weight in the nose, so it came down upside down. But it didn't break the egg. Joanna's was pretty heavy. Hers was based on the same assumption—the explosion principle—with infinite paper baffles and her egg in the center of this whole thing, surrounded by these paper baffles and these things were just for decoration. The idea again would be that this would of course explode, and these baffles would absorb the impact and the egg would pop out or something.

Did it work?

Yeah, it worked. Hers actually flew properly, you know, down and straight.
Except that we also learned that when you drop an egg onto a grassy surface it will stand up to quite a bit of abuse anyway. Kerry got a bunch of foam rubber and tied it together with rubber bands and tossed it off the roof. It hit and bounced two feet in the air and went clonk, and when they opened it up the egg was OK.
Actually, it would have been a lot more significant if we had tried cement. We had thought of trying to get the police helicopter to do some public service work and fly over the football field and drop these things one at a time onto the football field. I can't recall if anybody approached them or not, or whether they weren't available. . .
We thought we'd start a riot if the police helicopter were circling over, dropping things.

How many entries were there?

At least 10 or 12; there were a whole bunch.

And how many were successful? First of all, what

were the criteria of success?

Did you allow any hairline fractures or anything?

Would you say that the most successful projects were the simplest? The things that James is getting into are really kind of sophisticated, I mean to begin talking about machinery. Everything so far that you've done has been limited to working with materials that are easily available, such as cardboard, paper, things like that.

What kind of problems did you have to solve in the paper boat contest?

Was this your first design or did you experiment with it?

That the egg would survive.

We never had that problem, actually. No, either the egg broke or it survived intact. Someone did use a parachute in the end, and that worked really well. Half and half. Half made it and half didn't.

What happened later, what happened after the contest, was almost as important as the contest. Somehow or other people had gotten hip to eggs. Some of them who weren't in contact with any of the process came to school with their own eggs and started an egg war in the hall. A few of the eggs landed at the feet, at the very doorstep, of the "community relations" lady, who thinks that one of the greater indignities that can happen to befall you is to have someone throw an egg and have it land at your doorstep. She came storming over here and charged me with being responsible for this egg at her doorstep. If we hadn't gotten people thinking about eggs, she said, this would never have happened. I don't know what would have been at her doorstep, but it wouldn't have been an egg. I suppose she's never had an egg at her door. That was over very quick. It was probably the only thing that was really disturbing.

Yeah, I think the paper boat contest was the best and most spectacular of all the contests.

From the labor point of view it was pretty straightforward. The biggest problems came in bending these big tubes, and we broke most of the tubes 'cause we didn't know how to bend them. And we had a pretty good idea what we were going to do before we started working on it.

This was our first design, and we just made this in hope that it would work. We were reasonably certain that it would be water-tight. We toyed with the idea of making all these compartments watertight; in the event that we should get a puncture somewhere at least we would have enough time to get the heck out of the boat before it went down completely. Our other big problem was seating.

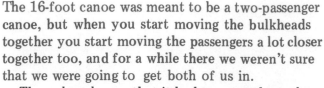

The 16-foot canoe was meant to be a two-passenger canoe, but when you start moving the bulkheads together you start moving the passengers a lot closer together too, and for a while there we weren't sure that we were going to get both of us in.

The only rule was that it had to carry the maker.

That's right. We were going to paper it with comic strips because it would be much more colorful than plain old black and white newspapers, and we stuck the rules on the top too. We were also worried about our center of gravity being too high, but I had nothing to worry about compared with the guys that built that other boat.

Yeah, that thing is so narrow.

How many people built canoes or boats?

There were a whole bunch.

One of them was papered inside with nude pictures and photographs—two, as a matter of fact.

Al Prince's class made one out of ice cream cartons. That was really good. It didn't break up.

Let's see, what were the rules? It had to be a boat; no rafts. Glue and string were acceptable. No surface coating that would dissolve and run off in water. No metal, plastic, wood, fiberglass, or rubber could be used in the construction. Submit questionable plans early to Morrison.

Morrison decided that wax was legal and nothing else was, 'cause he said wax was easy to obtain.

That's right, that was his rule. I wonder what would have happened if you couldn't use wax.

You would have had one hell of a mess in the swimming pool.

We had a mess anyway.

Have you got some idea of where you're going to go from here? Do you do the same things over again?

O.K., what happened was that because of the notoriety or publicity the class got I suddenly had three classes. It's difficult for one person; I think three people could generate ideas and somehow or other find the energy to handle three classes. I couldn't do it, but once it was institutionalized, on a large basis, with me still being seemingly responsible, the energy to promote them, to encourage them, to suggest things — it didn't work as well. I'll be happy in the Spring to go back to one class, where you start to provide health therapy for the school. All you're doing in a sense is doing things that other people can do in other classes and have done — in a math class, or science class or special class, or whatever. It seems crazy, and it's difficult for people to see sometimes what it has to do with being here, with the school. But hell, if you're not crazy, you're insane.

We carry our homes
within us
which enables us to fly

      —John Cage

AFTER WORDS

A book, too, is a winged moment, a point of consciousness in the author's life. When I read a book I always wonder about that moment, about the author, what it was and where it was that it all came about. All the things we create have a space, a place, a time, a context in which they happen and of which they speak. The space of this book is Berkeley with Colleen, a few weeks in the middle of a sabbatical, with friends, days in the wintry Sierras, moments shared with people close to us . . . lunches with Wally, where it all began . . . Salli and the horses and the rain on the land in Bodega . . . with De and Lindy and Marilyn in the fresh snow along Silver Creek . . . talk of amazing life games, kids, schools and fun writing projects to come with Jim and Carolyn . . . with Bill and Sarah and Cheeseburger reliving the frustrations and triumphs of a teacher's first year . . . Molly and Jon camped out in our living room gathering material for their China book . . . in Hal and Ellen's warm kitchen concocting cheese souffles before an afternoon hike in the "wilds" of Palo Alto . . . Arin's afternoon swim meets at Willard . . . planning the books that Bob and Tom are going to write (you're right Salli, everyone we know is writing a book!) . . . an afternoon bike ride to the marina with Lea and Alec, cheese and wine from greasy cups, watching Ron, el mechanico himself, taking his motor apart for the nth time . . . with Brooks, near-frostbitten hands tucked in our armpits trying to get the god-damned Svea to light in the cold of our Dewey Point snow-camp . . . photographing Dennis' class a couple of days after he and Lynn celebrated the arrival of Jason . . . realizing suddenly that my daughter Arin has become a young woman . . . bushwack-ing with Al through the hills of his Briones wilderness, talking of water wells and domes and joining up . . . runny camembert/avo-cado/banana sandwiches and champagne with Laird, Ron, and Frank . . . little Peter breaking his leg schussbooming off the top of Broadway . . . planning the trip to Mexico with Wendy and Reynaldo and little Luma . . . reading galleys for *The Human Expe-rience* and frantic phone calls to Richard in Boston . . . visiting Harry's seminar . . . reading Anais Nin, John Muir, Margaret Mead's *Blackberry Winter*, and Farley Mowat . . . rain, rain, rain . . . hilar-ious highs in the house on Broderick . . . discovering *feijoada* . . . and doing what I want to do.   *Berkeley, March 1973*

Covelo, October 1974, a Mendocino fall recalls Indian Summers in an Illinois childhood. Dusty-warm days of sun, Milky Way nights, huddle to the woodstove mornings. Sadako and Jim are the first to arrive, the smoke from the iron stove signals the begin-ning of a Yolla Bolly Press day. Arin and Brooks have left the tall grass and Eel River dips for red omnibuses, the Heath, and Parliament Hill. And with their help the cabin is ready. Its lamps are filled and the Sparkola waits for something more than the October chill (the winter's to be a bad one, the people of the Valley say). It's home now. The guitar on the wall promises some more after dinner sets with Frank and Sue. The months since the work of *Eggs* began have become a year and more, a time of adventures and decisions. Colleen and I have left McGee and Allston to be here with Carolyn, Jim, Binky, Moses, the horses, and our early, early morning acorn woodpecker, to feed tortillas and apple cores to a dusty Mr. Jackson and watch the deer in the Round Valley. The reward for the long wait has been a real design collaboration with Jim, happily not to end with *Eggs*, but to go on now with *The Backyard History* and the who-knows-what beyond.

DW

A LETTER FROM RASBERRY

David,

Remember I was writing out of a suitcase stored in the trunk of my trusty ole blue Plymouth when we first met? I came to Berkely to share tea and anecdotes. I was impressed with your wall of books about Asia and world history, education and philosophy; with your music; and your well-ordered work space. We communicated easily, our shared experiences of children and learning bouncing freely back and forth.

You were just finishing *The Human Experience* and were anxious to start another, looser book full of quotes, and projects, and the work of friends. You were going to create a total experience; I felt if you could you'd include your whole live school.

I left that day with the warm heady feeling of having met a new friend—a friend full of tenderness and concern for the young lives he touches each day in his classroom.

You came during the rain to my leaky tipi home to pick up our conversation in the form of an interview for the second *Rasberry* book; to invite me to share in the work of creating *Eggs and Peanut Butter*. I knew it would be an important, exciting project: an insight into change and structure, the magic of exploration and interaction—captured moments in an ordinary urban school in Oakland, California.

We spoke of the children's hunger for order and how it is our fear which causes us to impose rules and punishments, to be controlling and manipulative in the name of structure. It is we, their guides, who must learn to share our personal structures to help unveil the strategies of the wise among us so that students may have healthy models to draw upon; we, who must learn to provide an environment conducive to learning those skills with which our children may create their own inner structure. This self-recognition and giving of our own structure is crucial lest we unknowingly create the "Way to Be" in a desperate attempt to maintain law and order in our classrooms.

Hopefully we will not shield our young from the hard work of growing. Allowing children space to learn from each other, to view themselves in a supportive group context instead of coaxing them through the "right-answer maze" takes courage, being a most radical departure from the present-day teacher-student relationship. Influencing our students by providing them with working models of how people solve problems, helping them gain skills to survive, is our duty and our joy. The electric energy produced by learning with our students may cause the hair to stand up on the back of our collective necks, igniting that potential spark that dwells within all teachers.

You have created that book, David, and although your project is finished, I feel your work is just begun. For these pages are a tiny reaching-out—one half of a dialogue with teachers everywhere.

In our bones we teachers know what needs to be done, but those long-repressed feelings and intuitions have been tucked away in a somewhere bottom drawer along with ubiquitous teacher's manuals and forgotten lesson plans. *Eggs and Peanut Butter* will help put teachers back in touch with the rewards and joys of their profession. *Eggs and Peanut Butter* should be felt in every classroom in America.

 — 💙 *Salli Rasberry*